OVER THE HILL BUT NOT THE CLIFF

5 Strategies for 50+ Job Seekers to Push Past Ageism & Find a Job in the Loyalty-Free Workplace

LORI B. RASSAS

Part of *The Perpetual Paycheck* series

Other Books by Lori B. Rassas

The Perpetual Paycheck: 5 Secrets to Getting a Job, Keeping a Job, and Earning Income for Life in the Loyalty-Free Workplace

Employment Law: A Guide to Hiring, Firing, and Managing for Employers and Employees

DEDICATION

To DANICA, JAMIE, LOGAN, and DAVIS—
I know you will climb whatever hill you happen to come across.

CONTENTS

PREFACE

My most recent book, *The Perpetual Paycheck: 5 Secrets to Getting a Job, Keeping a Job, and Earning Income for Life in the Loyalty-Free Workplace*, provides job seekers with hands-on, specific strategies to navigate the loyalty-free workplace in all phases of their careers. While no one wants to hear that workplace loyalty is obsolete, the reality is that in today's work environment, more often than not, employment is based on short-term commitments. If you put in a full day's work on Monday, your employer is obligated to pay you for that time. As for Tuesday, nothing is guaranteed. The employer can tell you that your services are no longer needed, just as you can inform your employer that you intend to resign. That is what all of us face, and so the trick is to tailor your job search efforts to this new reality. Once you do that, you put yourself in a position to find a job, keep a job, and earn income for life in this new environment.

I am very grateful that *The Perpetual Paycheck* resonated with so many readers. Thanks to you, the book became an Amazon #1 best seller in three different job search categories.

Since the publication of *The Perpetual Paycheck*, many readers have asked whether the strategies I presented apply to individuals of all ages (yes), and whether I had any additional advice that specifically addresses the challenges faced by older candidates in their job search efforts (yes, again). The book you are about to read answers those questions and responds to other reader feedback I received. In addition, because the advice and strategies in this book go hand in hand with *The Perpetual Paycheck*, I have included an excerpt from *Paycheck* that I hope you will enjoy. (You will find these bonus materials at the end of this book.)

I am incredibly humbled by the manner in which my prior books have been received and I look forward to your continued input as I work on a number of future projects. Until then, I wish you the best of luck in your job search and have full confidence that you can and will achieve unprecedented success—regardless of which birthday is next.

—Lori B. Rassas

INTRODUCTION

AGEISM IN THE LOYALTY-FREE WORKPLACE

If you find yourself reading this book, you probably have worked for a number of years (or perhaps a number of decades) and plan on working for a number more. If you were to look back at your employment history, I am sure there were high points, when you achieved great success, and times when you were off track. You may have been passed over for a promotion, or not received a job offer after a few rounds of interviews. Perhaps you were laid off through no fault of your own, were terminated for behavior you now regret, made a lateral move, accepted a pay cut to take your career in a new direction, or took a leave of absence to tend to a personal matter. The life events that could have impacted your career are numerous, but like everyone else, your career trajectory includes a number of hills, roadblocks, valleys, bumps, or whichever metaphor best applies. And since you are reading this book, I would also assume you are ready to make a change—or perhaps being forced to make a change.

Now, if you asked me to describe the candidate most likely to find the best new position in the shortest period of time, would that person be an older candidate? Probably not. Then again, it would not be a recent college graduate, a candidate looking to move to a new geographic location, or someone looking to take their career in a new direction and work in a new industry.

No matter what your age or where you are in your career, you will face obstacles. Like death and taxes, they are inevitable. And, as you overcome one challenge (such as a recent college graduate struggling to get a few years of work experience under her belt), another one will surface (such as when that same person decides to move across the country when her fiancé is accepted to medical school there). You just need to identify the specific obstacles that impede your path and work your way past them.

Just as we will all face some obstacles in our career trajectories, all of us will also age—and there will likely be times when our qualifications are overshadowed by our age (and, more to the point, how hiring managers perceive our age). Fair or not, this happens one way or another in virtually every industry. When it happens, we are faced with two choices: We can see it as a cliff and rail against the system, or we can see it as just another hill to navigate along our workplace journey. The good news is that once you climb this hill, there is nothing to stop you from gaining speed and achieving levels of success you did not previously even contemplate.

I can appreciate the fact that ageism in the workplace is a hot-button issue. Break it down to its essence, however, and it is simply no different than any other career obstacle you need to overcome. Once you identify the challenges faced by older candidates, you will be in a better position to scale that hill and move on to the next challenge.

> "Just remember, when you're over the hill, you begin to pick up speed."
> CHARLES M. SCHULZ

If you have picked up this book, you are well on your way to acquiring some incredibly effective tools that will enable you to move up and over this hill. I know you may be frustrated, perhaps because you have responded to at least fifty ads for job openings, reached out to ten people for informational interviews, and scheduled a handful of meetings or job interviews. Despite all your efforts, you have yet to receive a job offer. Or maybe you have worked in the same job for a number of years, have continued to be passed over for promotional opportunities, and are concerned that it is just a matter of time before you are laid off. Or you might be changing jobs in the middle of your career, or you might be out of work for a reason that is no fault of your own.

Whichever scenario fits you best, I am fairly certain you have a very strong work ethic and are committed to remaining in the workforce. But I will also bet that you are having trouble fully committing to a robust job search because it seems like forever since your efforts produced any meaningful results. You might even think your age is the very thing that is holding you back.

If any of the above situations apply to you, even remotely, this is the book for you. I have spent a lot of time navigating the modern workplace and determining the best approaches with the greatest chances of success. This is my business: I am an employment attorney, human resources consultant, career coach, and negotiator. I provide guidance to executives, entertainment personalities, and working professionals at all stages of their careers. Plus, I have sat on the other side of the desk and have represented employers, so I understand how the workplace works from both sides. And, through this work, I have discovered a number of strategies that have enabled older job seekers to use their age—and all of the wisdom, skills, and experience that come with it—to their advantage to achieve unprecedented success.

The loyalty-free workplace is yours to conquer. With some basic knowledge about today's environment, and some new strategies designed to help you tackle it, before long you will find that hill behind you and a new horizon before you.

So, since we aren't getting any younger, it is time to get to work.

YOU CANNOT BE BLAMED FOR HOW OLD YOU ARE

As we move forward, understand one thing: If anyone is to blame for any negative perceptions related to age, it is certainly not you. The fact is, negativity associated with age is ingrained in our culture. Think of the billions of dollars we spend every year on beauty products and procedures designed to prevent or hide the signs of aging. The message is clear: Aging is something we should work to avoid.

The problem, of course, is that all of these products and procedures are built on a fallacy, because all of us are still going to age. As George Carlin once put it, "It's on our schedule."

And these negative perceptions should not come as a shock to any of us since we face them not just as we grow older but from a very young age.

©Glasbergen
glasbergen.com

— GLASBERGEN

**"My teacher says little girls can grow up to be anything they choose!
Why did you choose to be an old lady?"**

Consider how a child responds when a parent or grandparent makes an innocuous remark like "Oh, boy, I am getting old!" Does the little one say, "Yes, Grandma, you certainly are"? Of course not! Most children (or most anyone else, for that matter) are more likely to say the opposite: "You are *not* old!" or "No, you're not!"

Nevertheless, the message gets conveyed: young = good, old = bad. So, as you grow older, both in general and in terms of your career, do not be surprised if one day (1) you find yourself on the receiving end of some negativity related to your age, or (2) you have to engage in some strategic work to convince someone (such as a hiring manager) that none of the negative stereotypes related to age apply to you.

> "It's paradoxical that the idea of living a long life appeals to everyone, but the idea of getting old doesn't appeal to anyone."
> ANDY ROONEY

NOW, SOME GOOD NEWS

First and foremost, you are not alone. Each day, more than ten thousand baby boomers celebrate their sixty-fifth birthday, and this is expected to continue for decades to come. This well-publicized statistic means that there are tens of thousands of others in their forties, fifties, and early sixties who are right behind them. And not only are people aging, but many members of this vast population are looking for work. Some are unemployed through no fault of their own. Some are currently employed and looking for a change. Some are employed but are concerned that they will not be included in their company's future plans.

No matter what the circumstances, few of these candidates are ready to retire, and many are concerned about their financial future. Some are apprehensive about looking for a new job. Many are angry and frustrated because they believe that rampant age discrimination is the reason for their current situation.

In addition, many older job candidates tell me they are nervous about the process because they have not sent out a cover letter, updated a resume, attended a networking event, or gone on an interview in years (or, in many cases, decades). Some even feel out of their element because this is one of the first times in their working life, if not *the* first time, that they have ever been out of work or felt that their job was at risk.

No doubt, this is daunting—and I certainly empathize whenever I hear a client share a similar experience. At the same time, I cannot help but commend the candidate for being able to tell their story. Why? Because the truth is, very few people who are just now entering today's market-place will have the luxury of a career that gives them a sense of security for decades. In the loyalty-free workplace, where short-term commitments are the norm and jobs can end at any given time, most people will find themselves continuously engaged in the job search. Few expect to be in the same position for more than five years, let alone work in the same position or even with the same company until their fifties or sixties. So, in this regard, if you are embarking on your first true job search, or if you are back in the job market for the first time in thirty years, this is actually quite an accomplishment, for which you should be very proud.

PREPARE FOR THE WORST AND EXPECT THE BEST

For an older candidate starting to develop a job-search strategy, the best approach is to think of the development of an age-specific job search as the umbrella you tuck in your bag on a sunny day. It is not that you do not trust that the sun will continue to shine; you just want to be prepared if and when the storm hits.

This is the best strategic approach, because we may never know if our application was turned down, or if we did not get an offer after interviewing, because of our age. Nevertheless, we still have to approach the job-search process knowing that it *may* happen. This is no different than many other decisions we make in our lives. We purchase health insurance even though many of us may never need a major surgery. We purchase homeowner's insurance even though, thankfully, most of us will never be faced with the total loss of our home. However, just the possibility of its occurrence should motivate us to prepare for it.

Practically speaking, how do we do this? By casting a very wide net. After all, even if age discrimination is one reason why you are not getting the job offers and opportunities you deserve, it might not be the only one.

EMBRACE THE AGING PROCESS

Consider this: You wake up in the morning, swing your legs off the bed and stand up. Few people upon waking spend any time wondering whether their feet will hit the floor. Why? Because when you open your eyes, you know gravity is there, so you do not spend any precious time thinking about it.

This analogy applies to older candidates and their job-search process in two important ways. We can wake up each morning and worry about whether we will age. However, just like gravity is a constant, so is aging. Ten years from now, we will be ten years older than we are today. Whether we think about it or not, it will happen.

> "If you're always battling against getting older, you're always going to be unhappy, because it is going to happen anyhow."
> MITCH ALBOM

I have a friend who, in her late thirties, told our friends that she had been accepted into medical school and was going to become a doctor. We were all taken aback at this decision, especially since she had already achieved

> "I don't really have a choice. I'm getting older."
> ANNETTE BENING

career success in an unrelated field. In fact, one friend said, "Wow, that seems so depressing—she will be middle-aged and just starting out as a doctor." Almost instinctively, I replied, "There is no avoiding the fact that in ten years she will be middle-aged. So she might as well be a middle-aged doctor."

My point is that rather than spending our time, energy, and resources thinking about whether we are going to age, why not focus instead on something we can control: how to prevent the aging process from disrupting our stream of income.

YOUR AGE CANNOT HURT YOU, BUT LYING ABOUT IT WILL

Many of the strategies we will discuss relate to changing the way hiring managers perceive our age. This is quite different from lying about our age or trying to convince a hiring manager we graduated from college during the millennium when it was actually two or three decades before.

> Overheard:
> *Husband:* Does this outfit make me look younger?
> *Wife:* No, the outfit makes you look like a seventy-five-year-old in Lycra shorts.

It makes no sense to hide your age, because you can only hide it for so long. Even if you completely sanitized your resume, removing any evidence of the generation you associate with, at some point you will be sitting in front of a hiring manager who will see through your deception. While some employment experts say that once an older candidate gets that far in the process, their age is a nonissue, most hiring managers will beg to differ. After all, if you lied about your age just to get an interview, who is to say what else you have lied about and what else you will lie about if you get the job?

> "Old age isn't so bad when you consider the alternative."
> MAURICE CHEVALIER

The idea that gravity, just like the aging process, will continue to exist also relates to the discussion of ageism in the workplace. I have seen it count-less times through the experiences of my clients, colleagues, and some very close friends. Consider the social experiment set up by the AARP (the American Association of Retired People) (video of this experience is available at *http://www.aarp.org/disrupt-aging/stories/ideas/info-2016/ no-donuts-for-you-video.html*). This experiment involved a food truck with a prominently displayed sign that read "No One Over 40 Years of Age Will Be Served." As paying customers approached, a salesperson turned away customers who were clearly older than forty, saying sim-ply that the company "did not believe they were the right fit for their business," while telling those customers who were under forty that they had "exactly the vibe they were looking for." The responses varied. Some people accepted the conditions, while others said it was ridiculous. One person insisted that she wanted to buy the decadent treats not for herself but for her daughter—at which point, the salesperson said she would sell her the treats if the woman promised she would not eat them herself (and that she would step away from the truck as she waited for them to be prepared). The absurdity of this condition was not lost on anyone who witnessed the scene. Yet, this is precisely what is happening in our work-place. Every. Single. Day.

Age discrimination is real. It is present. It is illegal. It is wrong. The prob-lem, however, is that unlike in the very telling AARP experiment, the signs of discrimination are not as blatant, and neither is the connection between the adverse event and the person's age. In many cases, discrim-ination happens outside the public's view, and even when it occurs more openly, it is difficult to prove. This reality makes it less likely for a victim to invest the time, energy, and resources to pursue it.

From a practical standpoint, there are other reasons why you may not want to voice your concern that a company is engaging in discrimina-tion. For one, employers are overwhelmed with candidates and looking for reasons to exclude them; you do not want to make that decision any easier for them than it should be. Employers also hire cautiously, hoping to minimize the chances that they will bring a candidate with a nega-tive attitude, or someone who is angry, into the workforce. This is why I encourage clients to be positive and supportive of prospective employers, rather than confrontational and critical. After all, your main focus is to find a job that offers the stream of income you need to provide for yourself and your family.

Many of us may feel that "we know it when we see it," and if you are personally impacted by age discrimination, you may be angry and frustrated. However, if your goal is to find a job, when you are faced with this type of situation, the best response is to redirect your time, money, and energy toward employers who are less likely to engage in it (or hire you in spite of it).

This is not to minimize the importance of working to eradicate age discrimination and compel compliance with the law. But if your goal is to navigate the loyalty-free workplace successfully as an older employee, your best strategic move in terms of your job search is to be aware of the signals of potential age discrimination and work around them.

AGE IS NOT ALWAYS A FACTOR

Another reason not to blame ageism for why you are stuck in your job search is that, in some cases, it might not be the only reason for your situation. Or it may not have anything to do with your current situation.

> Account executive Davis Hocker, 56, is laid off after his company closed the satellite office where he had been working for close to three decades. Davis has been looking for a new opportunity for six months and has yet to receive an interview. During that time, he sent out over one hundred cover letters and resumes, hearing back from only eighteen prospective employers, who informed him that a more suitable candidate had been selected for the position. Davis concludes that age discrimination will prevent him from re-entering the workforce.

Davis' situation is all too common. But without further information, it is virtually impossible to determine whether his inability to land a new opportunity is strictly due to his age. For all we know, there may be other forces at work. Sometimes, a hiring manager will reject a candidate because he did not follow directions in the application process or sent in a poorly formatted resume. If one or both of these are true, Davis should be able to quickly and effectively address these issues and secure a new position. (We will be discussing some ways older candidates can make their resume work best in Strategy #1 and its postscript.)

Even if you were eliminated from consideration due to your age, do not automatically assume that the result would have been any different if you had been younger. Perhaps you interviewed poorly because you have not looked for a job in quite some time and were therefore out of practice. Perhaps you are relying on job-search techniques that worked well in the 90s but are no longer effective based on the realities of the loyalty-free workplace. Perhaps the prospective employer spoke with one of your references and they gave you a less-than-glowing recommendation. Perhaps you have the precise experience to fulfill the position, but the candidate who was hired had experience that was off the charts. Or maybe you were one of two finalists but lost out to the other candidate because she had a long-established personal relationship with one of the company's larger clients.

The fact is that any number of factors goes into a company's decision to hire a particular candidate. You may never know the true motivation for why they did not choose you.

Not only that, but even if your age *was* a factor, no hiring manager will ever tell you that—unless they want to subject themselves and the company to a legal discrimination claim.

The fact is that ageism may or may not play a role in a decision that results in your not getting the job offer. So, the question becomes, how do you properly prepare for this uncertainty? By using strategies that will overcome ageism if it plays a role but will not detract from your success in the event it does not.

"DRESSING" FOR SUCCESS

Imagine you hired a Hollywood stylist to help you become camera-ready for your walk down a red carpet. Naturally, you would want her to know all the basics to make you look fabulous on the big night. This includes the most appropriate fabrics and styles based on current trends, as well as whether it is a day or an evening event, the season, and the expected weather. Once the stylist gathers all of that information, she will use them as building blocks to create an age-appropriate outfit. After all, two people going to the same event (even if they are the exact same size, and have the exact same coloring) may be dressed completely different according to their age.

This is precisely how I approach the job-search advice you will find in this book. Our discussions about overcoming how prospective employers see your age will be tailored to a job search in the loyalty-free workplace. This, after all, is the employment environment we are all dealing with right now, so any effective strategies must take this into account. Once this foundation is laid, we will modify these strategies to ensure they address some of the biggest challenges faced by job seekers of an advanced age. Just like the Hollywood stylist, I want to be sure you possess not just *any* tools to survive in the loyalty-free workplace, but the *age-appropriate* tools that will enable you to truly thrive.

IT IS NEVER TOO LATE TO TAKE YOUR FIRST STEP

One other thing to keep in mind: No matter what your age, or where you are in your career or job-search process, you can do this. It is never too soon or too late to modify your strategies to achieve the greatest amount of success.

Financial advisors always emphasize the importance of starting to save for retirement at the earliest age possible. If you start saving in your twenties, you will increase the chances of achieving financial security during your retirement years. Even if you never thought about saving for retirement until you were fifty-five or sixty-five, it is not as if the advisor will say, "Sorry, too late, there is nothing I can do for you." More likely, the advisor will work with you so that you can make the best choices from this point forward. Since giving up on your job search is not an option, the only way to turn your fortunes around is to make a change today.

Before you start to limit your goals based on your late start, keep in mind that countless others have achieved great success later in life. Vera Wang did not start designing wedding dresses until she was forty. At fifty-seven, Chesley "Sully" Sullenberger III landed US Airways Flight 1549 in the Hudson River, saving the 155 passengers aboard; and at sixty-five, Colonel Harland Sanders started the KFC franchise. Ronald Reagan was fifty-five when he was elected to his first political office, and he became president at the age of sixty-nine, just a few weeks before his seventieth birthday. Even President Reagan was outdone by Nelson Mandela, who was seventy-six when he became president of South Africa.

> "It is a mistake to regard age as a downhill grade toward dissolution. The reverse is true. As one grows older, one climbs with surprising strides."
>
> GEORGE SAND

In addition, in a number of ways, the dynamics of the loyalty-free workplace actually favor older candidates. That may seem hard to believe at first, but once you understand the differences between the modern workplace and how things used to be, you will see a number of advantages that you will want to eagerly exploit.

COMPANIES COURT COMMITMENT

In the past, most employees followed a fairly standard path of career advancement, and employers made hiring decisions accordingly. People in their twenties and thirties (the age when most started their careers) selected the path that would provide them with a fairly steady income throughout their working lives. By the time they reached their forties, these candidates had usually specialized in some aspect of their industry, so they looked for promotional advancements that rewarded them for their years of service and enabled them to continue to climb the corporate ladder. While employees in their fifties also focused on their careers, more often than not, they also found themselves balancing those professional aspirations with personal needs such as caring for children, caring for aging parents, or thinking about retirement. And if you worked into your sixties, you would look for opportunities that promised job stability until retirement.

Long-term working relationships (lasting for perhaps twenty or thirty years) were viewed as mutually beneficial, and both employers and younger job candidates seemed eager to establish them. Conversely, companies were reluctant to hire older candidates, for fear that new hires above a certain age would not be in the job long enough to justify the

"Loyalty and enthusiasm are the two things
I value most in an employee. You're hired!"

time and expense it would take for training and acclimation to the company culture.

In today's workplace, however, the pendulum swings in a different direction. Younger candidates are unwilling to commit to any single company for more than three to five years, while older candidates are more likely to want and need a long-term and stable working relationship.

A number of factors have contributed to this dramatic shift. In some cases, older candidates may find themselves in a situation where their investments are not doing as well as anticipated. They may face uncertainty about healthcare costs and retirement and Social Security benefits, or they may be supporting their grown children longer than anticipated, for reasons related to the economy. In addition, with people living longer today, a sixty-year-old might plan on working in her new position for another ten years, which is considerably longer than what an employer today can expect from a junior candidate. All of this bodes well for older candidates, particularly because of the loyalty factor.

Many studies have shown that the harder you work for something, the more you appreciate it. Given the additional challenges that older candidates face today as they age, they will likely appreciate the job more than their younger counterparts. Why? Because they understand how challenging it is to secure a job once you reach a certain age. From an employer's standpoint, that means an older candidate today is more likely to stay in their job rather than face the prospect of another grueling search.

> "An enthusiastic young woman came into the nursing home where I work and filled out a job application. After she left, I read her form and had to admire her honesty. To the question 'Why do you want to work here?' she had responded, 'To get experience for a better job.'"
>
> —Deborah L. Bland

The generational divide can benefit older candidates by providing them with a strategic advantage against younger candidates. Whereas a candidate in his twenties might see a position as a stepping stone for a bigger and better job a few years down the road, a candidate in her fifties can assure a prospective employer that she is not a flight risk, but rather someone who will be committed to the company for years. So, when interviewing for a position with a history of high turnover, an older candidate can present himself in a way that highlights not only his experience (and how the company will benefit from it) but also his commitment to the company if he is hired. This, in turn, provides the employer with a form of stability that will ultimately benefit the company's clients and customers.

WHAT'S GOOD FOR THE GOOSE...

Of course it is possible that some younger candidates are looking for a long-term working relationship and that some older candidates are not interested in working into their seventies. This just further illustrates the point that age-related decisions, regardless of whether they exclude older candidates or younger candidates, may be based on stereotypes, have no validity, and eliminate qualified candidates who might possess the precise skills the employer is eager to find.

The fact is that just as there are employers who may be reluctant to hire older applicants, there are also employers who may be reluctant to hire younger candidates.

Sloane Sippler, 58, is looking for store managers for her new group of liquor stores. She is ideally looking for people who have management experience, who will be willing to remain in a mid-level manager role, and who will understand the importance of ensuring that everyone who purchases alcohol from the store is of legal age. When reviewing the resumes to determine which applicants should move forward in the process, Sloane concludes that an older candidate would likely be the best fit for this role.

In this case, there may be just as many younger candidates who are qualified for the vacancy as older candidates. Given her predisposition, though, Sloane will likely eliminate certain applicants on the basis of age. If you are an older candidate who knows about Sloane's recruiting goals, you have a significant edge.

The point is that to climb the hill that is in front of you, you will want to not only downplay any of the negative perceptions associated with your age, but also exploit any potential positives. So, when this situation arises, take advantage of it.

> "The good thing about being old is not being young."
> STEPHEN RICHARDS

Remember, your immediate goal is not to change the world or right any wrongs, but to land a job that will give you the income you need.

Now that you are armed with this knowledge, what do you do with it? The answer to that is threefold:

1. Understand that you are looking for a job in the loyalty-free workplace, so any strategies you use will have to be responsive to today's environment.

2. Acknowledge that even though age is just a number, the way hiring managers see your age often comes down to perception.

3. Recognize that there *are* job opportunities for older candidates, but you will have to be strategic to find them.

Once you understand these dynamics, you can start to learn how to present yourself in a way that will ultimately shift the conversation to where it belongs: to your qualifications for the position and the reasons why you are the best candidate to fill the vacancy. The first step in this process is to understand that the issue is not necessarily the number on your driver's license but what the number represents. This perception, and the impact it may have on your job-search process, is precisely what we will discuss next.

Pummeling this perception, and negating the impact it may have on your job-search process, are tackled next with Strategy #1.

STRATEGY #1

PUMMEL THE PERCEPTION

"Some guy said to me:
'Don't you think you are too old to sing rock 'n' roll?'
I said: 'You'd better check with Mick Jagger.' "
—*Cher*

Most companies start and move through the recruitment process with the goal of whittling down the applicant pool to a manageable number of candidates by "objectively" weighing the pros and cons of each candidate's application. Unfortunately, this initial review (and, really, a number of reviews that occur as the process unfolds) has the potential to place older applicants at a significant disadvantage. This is because the most common reservation about hiring older candidates has nothing to do with their actual age, but *what their age represents.*

What do I mean by this? Imagine an older person going about their day. Is that person sitting up straight or slouching? Is she walking slowly with a cane or a walker, or jogging on a beach? Is she reading a book with her feet up or dancing on a cruise ship? Does she use a landline or an iPhone? Is she wandering aimlessly or moving quickly toward a targeted destination?

Think of the verbs and adjectives you used to describe your picture. Did they evoke images of slow, inactive, and complacent, or fast, active, and eager?

Now imagine you are the hiring manager. If your image of an older candidate skews more toward "slow, inactive, and content," you have to decide whether such an individual is the best choice to represent the company in the position you are trying to fill.

GRAY HAIR IS GRAY HAIR

Let me give you an example. I had a childhood friend who turned gray prematurely. By the time we were juniors in high school, she had a full head of gray hair. She often talked about the time, money, and effort it took to regularly color her gray locks, until at one point she just decided to forgo those efforts. The bright side, she joked, was that she no longer had to fear the sight of a few gray strands. Sure, from time to time, someone would make a comment, but most of the time her gray locks were a non-issue and never interfered with anything we ever tried to do. And, I can assure you that, whenever we applied for seasonal jobs during the summer, my friend never complained about failing to get a job as a short-order cook, a lifeguard, or a retail sales clerk because of the color of her hair. Why? Because hiring managers do not eliminate candidates on the basis of gray hair—gray hair is just gray hair. What hiring managers do consider, whether consciously or unconsciously, is what the gray hair represents.

Right or wrong, gray hair on a candidate who is sixty or older may represent someone who no longer has the drive to work full time, or who may have health problems now or in the near future, or who has limited technological knowledge. For my eighteen-year-old friend, however, gray hair represented none of that. First, nothing on her resume suggested she was an older candidate whose resume should not be considered. And second, once she met with the hiring manager, she came across as a vibrant, chatty, larger-than-life teenager who could sell a hot dog to a vegetarian.

> **"All our knowledge has its origin in our perceptions."**
> LEONARDO DA VINCI

WIPE OUT THE PERCEPTIONS

Now that you know the negative perceptions that may be inferred from your age, the next step is to figure out how to overcome those obstacles so that they do not impact your job-search process. This means examining each perception and working to send a clear message that it does not apply to you. If hiring managers perceive older candidates as tired and unmotivated, you must "make over" that image by presenting yourself as a candidate who is energetic, motivated, and capable of making an immediate and valuable contribution to the company.

©Glasbergen / glasbergen.com

"Of course I think about death. I'd like
to die young at a very old age."

The fact is, the moment the hiring manager picks up your application, you start to leave an impression. Your job is to make sure that the only impressions the hiring managers have are those that see you in the job, working alongside them.

Consider how a real estate agent tries to sell you a house. They do not merely show you pictures of a home—instead, they walk you through it, trying to get you to imagine sitting around the kitchen table with your family, hosting guests in the living room, and unwinding in the master bedroom after a long day at work. Similarly, if you want to make the sale, so to speak, you want the hiring manager to close their eyes and visualize you in the position.

"Youth is a gift of nature, but age is a work of art."
GARSON KANIN

Does this mean that you need to start running half-marathons in your fifties so that you can match the vigor of a candidate in their twenties? No. All I am saying is that a hiring manager will likely look for a candidate who can attend, and possibly even lead, important meetings with the energy, enthusiasm, and commitment necessary to close the deal. Not only do you want the hiring manager to see you as that candidate, you want them to smile at the notion of you whizzing by coworkers who are twenty years your junior.

Remember, everything you do in the job-search process—from selecting which opportunities to pursue, to drafting your cover letter and resume, to what you wear and how you behave in an interview—is geared toward eliminating any preconceived notions a prospective employer has about your age. Is that unfair? Perhaps, but look at it this way: The more you do to dispel these preconceived notions, the more level the playing field becomes—and the less your age becomes a factor. And assuming you make that all-important first cut, you want to immediately make it clear that you are the ideal fit for the position because of the immense value you immediately bring to the table, and your age will do nothing to detract from this benefit.

> "You can't help getting older, but you don't have to get old."
> GEORGE BURNS

THE CINDERELLA FIT IS THE FOUNDATION

When working with clients, I often focus on what I call the "Cinderella fit," which is the notion that employers want what employers want. If you are not the perfect fit for the vacant position, an employer is not likely to seriously consider your application. In the past, when employers had plenty of staff, they could afford to hire a candidate who was a close fit (as far as qualifications go), but not a perfect one. In some cases, employers might have even hired people who were clearly *not* qualified for the position, but who had enough potential that they would "find a spot for them."

The fact is, today's workplace is loyalty free and employers are focused solely on their own goals and their own interests. And, because of this, the luxury of hiring people for their *potential* contribution is a luxury that no longer exists. "Pretty good" or "close enough" will not cut it anymore. With more qualified people than ever competing for fewer jobs, companies adopt an incredibly selective approach to their hiring decision. Like Prince Charming, prospective employers are looking for the one person who is the perfect fit for that glass slipper—and if it does not fit (or if you say something during the interview that suggests you would be a bad fit), they almost always have a stack of other qualified candidates to consider instead of you.

If you are granted an interview, you must show the prospective employer right then and there that you know all of the "tricks" necessary to excel at the job. In the loyalty-free workplace, you cannot be a dog who *might* learn new tricks. You have to be ready to hit the ground running and provide an immediate, measurable benefit to your prospective employer.

If you are in a place in your career where you have the precise experience the hiring manager is looking for (both in terms of the number of years of experience and the requisite skill set), you need to let him know that. Not only that, to the extent that you have unique skills that set you apart from other candidates, you need to point that out to the hiring manager so that he sees you, and only you, as the perfect fit. Once you do that—once you find and focus on positions for which you fit the glass slipper (at least on paper)—you can start to exploit the benefits of being an older candidate, while also minimizing any characterizations that can eliminate you from consideration.

> "Aging is an inevitable process. I surely wouldn't want to grow younger. The older you become, the more you know; your bank account of knowledge is much richer."
> WILLIAM HOLDEN

The good news is that being an older candidate means that you can provide the employer with immediate and measurable benefits. For one, given your knowledge and experience, you can perform the job efficiently (which, in turn, means that a prospective employer will not have to spend time, money, and resources on getting you up to speed). Along the same lines, unlike younger candidates, a more experienced candidate will need less supervision. Not only that, but by virtue of your experience you might be able to train younger coworkers once you are hired. That frees the employer of this time-consuming obligation, while enhancing your value to the company. Plus, being an older candidate, you have a track record of results. Unlike a younger candidate with great potential who *might* be able to deliver, you can present yourself as a proven veteran who *has, can,* and *will* deliver.

In addition, if you are like most people in your forties or fifties or sixties, your children (if you have any) are probably all grown up and on their own. That means a prospective employer would not have to worry about possible unexpected absences because your child is sick or daycare is not available that day. You may be more willing to accept a flexible schedule, perhaps working in the evenings or an occasional weekend—which, again, is a benefit that a younger candidate with a child in kindergarten may not be able to so readily deliver.

Why should you tackle the preconceived notions related to aging within the context of the Cinderella fit? Because an individual whose candidacy evokes images of an aging frail candidate counting the months or even years until retirement is less likely to land the vacant position than an active, vibrant, and eager candidate who is committed to learning about a prospective employer's needs and meeting them. Therefore, we need to examine each of the negative perceptions that are often associated with older candidates and make a conscious effort to ensure that the prospective employer is certain those elements in no way apply to you.

SMALL TALK MAKES A BIG DIFFERENCE

When providing advice to candidates of all ages, I stress the importance of always staying on point when responding to questions posed by a hiring manager. That goes for whether the questions are posed within the context of a formal interview or as part of a preliminary phone call after the manager has reviewed your application. Every answer you give, regardless of the question, should be tied to a specific job task or qualification for the position for which you have applied. The reason why is simple: Because you cannot assume that a preliminary phone call will lead to a formal interview, you have to make the most of the phone call and approach it as if it were an interview. So when an employer asks you to tell them a little about yourself, rather than talk about your husband and your two grown children and your pets and how you live in a neighborhood that reminds you of where you grew up, zero in on workplace experiences that best illustrate how you can make an immediate and valuable contribution to the position.

Now suppose that, after hearing you make your pitch on why you would be the best choice for the job, the hiring manager asks you what sort of hobbies or interests you have (or some other question that does not appear to relate to the vacant position). Some responses are more effective than others, because, in asking the question, the hiring manager is evaluating whether or not you are a good fit for the company.

> "Youthfulness is about how you live, not when you were born."
> KARL LAGERFELD

How does this relate to age and the perception of age? Say we have two candidates: Marge, who is in her twenties, and Aaron, who is in his fifties. If Marge were to tell the hiring manager that her outside interests include reading and sail boating, that likely would not impact her candidacy one way or another. But, because most people consider sail boating and reading to be sedentary activities, if Aaron were to give the same answer, that could harm his candidacy because it feeds into the very stereotype the older applicant should be working to overcome.

Remember, you want to present yourself as a vibrant, active candidate, not one who is counting the days until you are able to retire. A more strategic response from Aaron would be to reference his interests in running, jet skiing, or even skydiving—all of which are active hobbies that reinforce the images of a vibrant candidate. Or, if Aaron's only real hobby is sailing (but he happens to be broad shouldered and look about ten years younger than his age would suggest), he can talk about the strenuous upper-body workout he gets from working the sails every time he is out on the water, particularly on a windy day.

Now, what if Aaron's favorite pastime happens to be reading (which, again, most would perceive to be sedentary and "non-vibrant")? If he is a voracious reader who completes several books a week along with several industry publications, Aaron can use that to show the hiring manager that he is mentally sharp, eager to learn, and well versed in industry trends.

You should take the same approach to answering questions related to family dynamics. Let us say Aaron happens to have grandchildren— an image that, like it or not, also plays into certain stereotypes about age. In telling the hiring manager how much he enjoys spending time with his grandchildren, Aaron might mention what fun he had when he took them to Europe last summer, or how much he enjoyed riding the latest roller coaster with them. Activities such as these present Aaron as a high-energy, active candidate who continues to live life to the fullest, and who will not have difficulty waking and reporting to a high-pressure job each day.

This should go without saying, but in no way am I suggesting that you conjure up stories of grandiose adventures of hiking in third world countries if, in fact, you live more of a sedentary life. Instead, I am encouraging you to draw on your full arsenal of experiences and present them in the best possible light for the position for which you are applying.

ABANDONED INTEREST IN LEARNING

Another stereotype that older candidates must overcome is the perception that once they have reached a certain age or certain point in their career, they no longer care about learning. In the job-search process, this stereotype becomes problematic because so many hiring managers either intentionally or unintentionally approach older applicants with three fears: (1) you have no desire to learn new skills that may be necessary to succeed in the new position; (2) while you may have the desire to learn new skills, being of a certain age you may no longer have the capacity or patience to master them so that you can succeed in the new position; or (3) because you have been accustomed to performing certain tasks in the same way for an extended period of time, you may be set in your ways and, therefore, unwilling to adapt to a new work environment.

Now, if we were to be honest, the first concern is valid in some respects. There are times in our life when learning is a priority, and times when it is no longer a central focus. When we are in college, our entire working lives are ahead of us and we are eager to learn about the world. After graduating from college and perhaps earning a second degree, we may reach a position where we want to shift our interest in learning about new things to using the knowledge we have acquired to earn money and establish our careers.

> "Anyone who stops learning is old, whether at twenty or eighty. Anyone who keeps learning stays young."
> HENRY FORD

That said, most hiring managers know that, when push comes to shove, some candidates would be both willing and able to learn new skills on the job if they were asked to do so. Problem is, most prospective managers tend to offer this benefit of the doubt to younger candidates only. Meaning, if an older candidate creates the impression that he is not interested in learning a new approach to the job, the hiring manager will take that to mean that he has reached the point of his career where he is no longer motivated to continue to grow.

More troubling, however, is the perception that older candidates not only lack an interest in learning, but also lack the ability to learn. Depending on the circumstances, this can also make the hiring manager think that the older candidate's skills are outdated.

> Jeffrey Scott, 28, and Sabrina Saunders, 53, have substantially similar qualifications, including their academic qualifications, both having graduated in the top third of their class at the same well-respected academic institution. The deciding factor in extending the offer to Jeffrey is that, since he graduated from college five years ago, he would be more likely to possess relevant and updated knowledge than Sabrina, who graduated thirty years ago and would most likely have a knowledge base that is stale and outdated.

It is very possible that both Jeffrey and Sabrina have what it takes to succeed in the vacant positions. Not only that, the fact that Sabrina has more years of relevant workplace experience may have actually made her the better choice to fill the position. The perception, however, could lead to a hiring manager's decision to bring in Jeffrey for an interview instead of Sabrina, particularly if their skill set is similar. Since Sabrina cannot alter her graduation date, she would have to impress upon the hiring manager her willingness and eagerness to continue to learn. Not only would that show the prospective employer that she has the foundational knowledge for the position, it would indicate her ongoing commitment to keeping that knowledge current so that it is on par with the knowledge acquired by other, younger candidates. In doing so, Sabrina shifts the focus away from education so that workplace experience is the deciding factor as to who ultimately gets the job.

Now, many career experts advise older candidates to remove the graduation dates and dates of employment from their resume, in order to downplay the fact that they are older and that the information acquired

**"I need to present a younger, hipper image.
Can I get my résumé pierced and tattooed?"**

through the academic portion of their career may no longer be relevant. Removing graduation dates from resumes is becoming more common, even for younger candidates, and this is a strategy you might want to consider. However, I do not believe in this approach as it relates to your dates of employment. Why? Because removing information that suggests you are older actually tends to bring *more* attention to your age due to its absence.

Instead, I suggest a more targeted strategy that gets to the crux of the problem: Rather than deleting information that might bring attention to its absence, add information that counteracts the negative perception that your graduate date might suggest.

Remember, the issue is not that you graduated from college twenty-five years ago. The issue is what this graduation date represents: the possibility that your knowledge is stale and not updated to reflect modern society. So if you went back to school to earn an advanced degree (or perhaps a certificate program of some sort), add that in a prominent spot on your resume. If you have attended any conferences in the past year, put those down, too. And on the off chance you have been putting off taking those continuing education courses, now is just as good a time as ever to start.

It is one thing to tell a prospective employer that you possess the requisite knowledge to complete the essential jobs tasks. It is another thing to be able to show them. Obtaining current and relevant knowledge and making sure it is showcased not only demonstrates your ongoing willingness to learn, but is another way of presenting yourself as precisely the type of vibrant, energetic, and active candidate that the company is looking to hire.

> "There is a foundation of youth: it is your mind, your talents, the creativity you bring to your life and the lives of people you love. When you learn to tap this source, you will truly have defeated age."
> SOPHIA LOREN

DO NOT BE UNCOACHABLE

Another reason it is important to emphasize your continued willingness to learn is because it will also show a prospective employer that you have the capacity to embrace change. This is important because another pervasive perception is that older candidates who have significant experience will be reluctant to adopt a new approach to completing a particular task they have performed for years. Perhaps you roll your eyes when a grandparent or older customer makes a comment that would generally be considered unacceptable (or "politically incorrect"). Even if we express this mild disapproval, we tend to give Grandpa a free pass simply because of the adage that if a person has not changed by now, they never will.

This, of course, is not the type of message you want to convey in your job search, and you have to be particularly aware of this potential obstacle if you have years of experience and have worked for a particular employer for an extended period of time. You will want to avoid suggesting to a prospective employer that you are committed to a certain way of doing things. Why? Because even if your way is perfectly aligned with how the employer currently conducts his business, you need to show that you are flexible to assuage the employer's concern that you will be either unwilling or unable to conform to the company's practices. (In professional sports, they would call you "uncoachable" and put you on irrevocable waivers.) Depending

> "Old minds are like old horses; you must exercise them if you wish to keep them in working order."
> JOHN ADAMS

upon your level of resistance (or perceived level of resistance) to learning new ways to do the work, a prospective employer may determine it will be more effective to train a candidate with no experience how to complete a task in the way they want it done than to spend the time and money in training to get you to come around. This means that any benefit to hiring you on the basis of your vast experience will have fallen by the wayside.

Remember, your goal is to deflate any preconceived notions about you, your age, or your experience that can prevent you from getting the job offer. You want to portray yourself as a candidate who is willing and able to continue to learn, apply what you learn, and be open to doing whatever your employer or your boss believes is in the best interest of the company. This is particularly important if you end up with a boss who is younger than you.

REMEMBER WHO'S BOSS

When helping clients navigate their various employment issues, I often emphasize that while your business card may have the company's name on it, you work for your boss. Your primary job is to make your boss shine, which, in turn, will benefit you. It is human nature to wonder how someone twenty years our junior has managed to pass over us. However, like many other components of the hiring process (and even the modern workplace), this is simply another reality that you may have to face if you want the job for which you have applied. Put another way: Age is a number, but in this situation it is not the number that matters. The only numbers that you should care about are those that appear on your paycheck every week.

Another thing to bear in mind: You may not be the only one who is hung up over age. It is quite possible that your prospective boss (or, for that matter, the hiring manager) may be just as uncomfortable with interviewing someone who is older than them. If you sense that balloon is in the room, your job, again, is to puncture it. Manage those apprehensions by showing your prospective boss that she can work with you. Otherwise, she will shake your hand and move on to another candidate.

If you are in an interview and there are younger people in the room, acknowledge them and show them the same respect that you would expect from them if the roles were reversed.

> When Georgia Avril, 55, reaches out to hiring manager Ben Felder, 34, to confirm the time and location of her interview, his assistant explains that he is not yet in the office, but she will confirm the details by e-mail by late morning when Ben arrives in the office. When Georgia goes to the interview that week, she cannot help but be frustrated by the fact that if she receives the offer, she will be working for a boss who lacks a strong work ethic.

When you find yourself in a situation when you are interviewing with a younger boss, remember that just as you do not appreciate the fact that hiring managers are judging you by negative stereotypes related to age, it is unlikely that your younger boss would appreciate you engaging in the same evaluation of their work performance. For all you know, Ben was working through the night and just went home for a change of clothes or he had a meeting outside the office. Instead of focusing on the worst-case scenario, why not consider another option: that your future boss has a strong work ethic, is incredibly supportive, and will enable you to soar to new heights. And, even if your initial reaction is accurate, you should not let it distract from your primary goal, which is to get the job offer.

To accomplish this result, try to focus on establishing a connection that will bond you with your perspective boss regardless of any preconceived notions. Let that person know that you can learn from them and you will have no problem accepting their recommendations as to how you can improve. Ask for feedback or for their opinions. Explain how you view the relationship between the role you are interviewing for and the other members of the team, then ask the manager (or whoever is conducting the interview) whether she agrees with your assessment. Conduct yourself on the interview as if it were a typical day on the job. That means deferring to the interviewer when appropriate and being receptive and responsive to any feedback. Just as you would not tell a boss who is older than you how much better you are, or how much you can teach them, refrain from doing this with a younger boss.

If you have previously worked for a younger boss, incorporate that into the interview, as an example of how you have a successful track record of following the direction of a younger boss. If you have never worked for a younger boss, but have worked for companies that value new and innovative ideas (and an open mind for receiving and implementing them), look for an appropriate opening and drop that into the conversation. If you have been in a position where you benefitted from the knowledge of former coworkers who were more junior than you, work that into the conversation as appropriate.

> Ed Buckner, 61, interviews for a position as a marketing manager with prospective boss Daniel Alder, 33. When Daniel mentions that one of the company's priorities is to expand the customer base, Ed explains that he worked on a similar expansion effort in his prior role, which resulted in the company gaining a market share in areas that were not even on their original target list. Ed added that a number of his former colleagues who had recently worked in third world countries when they studied abroad in college likewise helped that company attract those new customers by appealing to cultural differences that their competitors were unaware even existed.

If neither situation applies in your case, you can always talk generally about the importance of working and supporting the members of your team. Just refrain from saying anything that could highlight your age differences.

> Jessica Reeves, 55, is invited to the third and final round of interviews with Eric Raner, 34, who would be her boss if she is hired into the new position. Aware of the company's concern related to employee turnover, Jessica decides to ask about opportunities to grow within the company over the long term. In response, Eric explains that he started at the company in the mailroom, and in a few short years was able to bring in a number of lucrative clients to the company and was subsequently promoted into his current vice-president position. Jessica remarks that Eric "looks quite young to be a vice-president" and is incredibly accomplished for his age.

It is quite possible that Jessica meant her comment to be a compliment (and for all we know, Eric may have taken it that way). Even so, she would have been wise not to make that particular remark. For one, Eric might also interpret this comment to mean that Jessica is resentful for not achieving this level of success herself. In which case, he might conclude she would be uncomfortable working for him.

More important, however, is the fact that by referring to Eric's youth, Jessica is basically drawing attention to her own age, which was what she should have been trying to prevent in the first place.

Age should have no place in the hiring process at all. That goes for old age, young age, or middle age. Any references to it should, therefore, be avoided. That means, among other things, not telling a potential boss how much she reminds you of your daughter, and avoiding any statements that start with "when I was your age…." Just as you want your application to be judged on your qualifications (and not your age), you should not judge the interviewer or prospective boss by their age. In an ideal world, age should not come into play in the discussion.

THE DEVIL IS IN THE DETAILS

While we are on the subject of taking direction, another stereotype that works against candidates of a certain age is the perception that an older candidate might be unwilling to do some of the more mundane tasks associated with the position. When first entering the job market, candidates are usually ready, willing, and able to do whatever it takes to get the job done. As we move forward in our careers, however, we may be less inclined to do so, simply because we like to think that we have already paid our dues and that there are many more useful ways to utilize our experience.

Of course, every candidate, regardless of their age, will tell a job interviewer that they are "willing to do what it takes to get the job done." That said, human nature being what it is, a hiring manager is more likely to believe that statement when a younger, less experienced candidate says it, versus an older, more experienced one.

How do you thwart that perception? By paying attention to every detail as you move through the job-search process, even the most mundane ones.

For example, some job candidates do not spend a lot of time preparing for interviews, choosing instead to do the minimum amount of research necessary. Knowing that, it is in your best interest to thoroughly research the people with whom you expect to interview. That includes doing some homework on the company itself (and its competitors), as well as finding ways to pose questions during the interview that show that you did your homework. An easy way to do this is by connecting with the company on LinkedIn. This will give you some basic information on the size of the company, its different offices (which might provide other opportunities for you, in case the company sees you as a viable candidate, but not for the position for which you have applied), its decision makers, and recent news postings. This will also give you an idea of the company's priorities, in terms of current projects and which accomplishments it wants to tout. In the event you are not comfortable using LinkedIn and other basic Internet research tools to gather information, this would be a good time to develop or brush up on these skills. At the very least, it will dispel any notion the hiring manager may have about your technological skills, another misconception that older candidates face, which we will discuss later in the chapter.

On top of this, you want to write thank you notes after each interview, making sure to spell the names and titles of the interviewers correctly. This does not take more than a few minutes, but it can go a long way toward impressing upon the prospective employer that you really are willing to do whatever is necessary to get the job done correctly.

And speaking of little things: Do not wait until the last minute to print your resume, only to realize on the morning of your interview that you need a new ink cartridge. I cannot tell you how many resumes I have seen eliminated right away simply because the print was less than sharp (and, therefore, hard to read). Along the same lines, be sure that your cover letter is addressed to the correct person and their name is spelled correctly, and check and double check your resume for misspellings and other grammatical errors. If you print your own business cards, use good stock paper (believe it or not, I know someone who once lost out on a job because the prospective employer said his business cards looked "cheap and unprofessional"). Or, if you are considering using one of those websites that offer free business cards, be sure there is nothing written on the card that indicates it was printed for free (I have a colleague who was eliminated from consideration for that very reason!).

While it is true that oversights such as these may be detrimental to any job candidate, they can be fatal for older candidates, simply because they play into the stereotype of "not willing to go the extra mile."

WHEN TECHNOLOGY IS A CATCH-22

Now, before we move on to the interview itself, a word about computer skills. Aside from the fact that you will need these skills to gather the information that will enable you to compete with other candidates in the hiring process, there is a perception among hiring managers that older candidates either do not have or are not willing to develop the technological skills necessary to thrive in the modern workplace. Therefore, using technology throughout all aspects of your job-search process, from sending out your resume and application to preparing for a job interview, can go a long way toward dispelling that notion. Not only that, it will show potential employers that there is no difference between your level of skills and those possessed by any younger applicants.

There is no doubt that individuals born in recent years are at an advantage because they have grown up in a technology-infused world, unlike most older candidates, who likely were introduced to technology at a later age. Nevertheless, this is another situation where you have to level the playing field. While everyone knows a handful of people who proudly exclaim that they do not own a computer nor do they use e-mail, it is simply unfathomable to think that someone who was born in the recent past would ever make such a proclamation.

This negative perception related to technology has two parts. The first relates to an unwillingness or inability to learn new skills (a topic we have already discussed). The second issue is a Catch-22: Even if you are willing to obtain new skills, that is not enough to land you the job offer (or even an interview) because most employers do not want to train you—they would rather you walk in, ready to go from day one. That part of the equation, of course, is directly tied to the idea of the Cinderella fit. In

**"Any chance you could learn PowerPoint
before your next presentation, Jim?"**

other words, if you do not already have the basic technological skills the position requires, you will not get the job regardless of your age.

Now, is it possible to eradicate all negative perceptions related to hiring older candidates as you go through your job search? The answer, unfortunately, is no. People being people, there is no way to predict for sure what can creep into a hiring manager's mind at any stage of the process. All you can do is be relentless in removing any obstacles that could possibly suggest that you are not the perfect fit. Along the way, remember that every person you approach in your job-search process works in the same loyalty-free workplace that you are in. This will impact how you go about each step in the process, from writing your cover letter and resume to taking part in interviews.

> "Age does not matter:
> an open mind does."
> TIMOTHY FERRISS

ACKNOWLEDGE WHAT YOU DO NOT KNOW BUT NEED TO LEARN

Quite often when I first meet with prospective clients who are of a certain age, they tell me how overwhelmed they are because they have no idea how to draft a cover letter, write a resume, or participate in an interview. More often than not, I usually respond, "That's not surprising. Why would you?"

Think about it. When you call your plumber, do you start by telling him how frustrated you are over your inability to snake a drain? Probably not. Instead, you would tell him what your problem is and ask how soon he can come out. Even if you did vent about your inability to snake a drain, the plumber is not likely to hold that against you. After all, your lack of knowledge in areas such as these is what secures his future income.

The fact is, writing a cover letter and resume and participating in interviews are no different than any other skills you may acquire during your working life. Your acumen in these areas will likely depend upon how many times you have engaged in a job search and, perhaps, the nature of your work. Meaning, if you make your living as a mechanic (or any other profession in which writing is not a big part of the job), you are more likely to need assistance writing a cover letter than an individual who has worked as an administrative assistant.

The same holds true if, being of a certain age and having held down the same position for a number of years, it has been a while since you last updated your resume or actively looked for a job. Deciding how to best present yourself can often make the difference between a cover letter and resume that results in a job interview (and an eventual job offer) and one that ends up in the slush pile.

If you find the thought of doing this yourself as daunting as repairing your own drain, you might consider reaching out to a professional resume writer. Besides helping you showcase your expertise, a professional resume writer can assist you in other ways. Suppose you are looking for a job in a new industry. A professional resume writer would likely know how to best highlight the short-term position you held in that industry—something that might not be as prominently displayed were you looking for a position in the same industry where you had worked for the past two decades. Depending on who you hire, and the training and skills the writer possesses, a good resume writer might also be privy to industry trends, and, therefore, be able to highlight your skills so that your qualifications shine.

Since we operate in a world of LinkedIn, search engines, and online databases, a trained professional resume writer will also know which keywords will most likely be identified by hiring managers, recruiters, and employers as they search for appropriate candidates.

These may seem like little things—but as the saying goes, they mean a lot. Besides, details such as these (as well as having a trained resume writer make sure that your letter has no grammatical errors) are yet another concrete way of showing a hiring manager or prospective manager that you really are willing to do what it takes to get the job done in just the right way.

Finally, if you decide to work with a resume writer (or any other professional, for that matter), do your due diligence before making your final selection. Just because Rosie's Resume Service says their employees have all worked in human resources, that does not mean they have sourced resumes or have any firsthand experience interviewing candidates. In addition, just as no two industries work in quite the same way, the foundational elements of a resume may vary depending upon the industry as well as the type of position and the level of positions for which you are applying. Your cousin may have helped dozens of senior executives land new positions, but she may have no idea of the current trends related to the job market for middle managers.

Similarly, if you have a recruiter in your network, you might want to go ahead and see if they would be willing to review your resume. Just be sure they have experience in your industry and with job seekers at your level. A recruiter that specializes in jobs in the financial industry will have a very different skill set than recruiters that place professionals in the medical, technological, or engineering fields. Also, remember that recruiters rarely present "cold" resumes—meaning, it is unlikely they will present any resume to their clients unless they already know what the client is looking for. You want to work with someone who can revise your resume so that it can be used for a general job search, which is a different skill set than knowing how to revise it to match a specific vacancy.

The same care should be used when asking a friend or family member to review your job search materials.

> Payroll specialist Maya Devler, 59, asks her daughter, Lexie Bachen, 33, to review her resume before she submits it with her online application. Lexie is the manager of one of the country's largest chains of online bookstores.

There is nothing wrong with Maya asking her daughter for job search advice. But what if it has been ten years since Lexie last looked for a job? Unless she has actively stayed on top of changes in the job-search process, Lexie may have no idea how the modern workplace operates. Even if Lexie's knowledge is current, it may relate to an industry that has different standards and priorities than the one in which Maya is seeking a new position. On top of that, she may have little, if any, of the specialized experience that is required when working with older candidates. The takeaway here is that while you may benefit from some job-search assistance, make sure the assistance is on target with precisely what you need. Do not settle for *any* help, but rather expend the necessary efforts to ensure that any help you do receive moves you closer to your goal and does not detract from it. Regardless of whether you decide to seek out or forgo professional help, see Postscript: Covering the Bases of Your Resume and Cover Letter, for some foundational knowledge about how to approach this process.

ESTABLISH A STRONG SOCIAL MEDIA PRESENCE NOW SO YOU CAN TAP INTO IT LATER

As you are reading this book and starting to work on these preliminary materials, do not forget to work on your social media presence—and if you have no social media presence, now is the time to get it up and running *before* you start applying for jobs. Why? For many of the same reasons we have discussed. If a prospective employer has any concerns about your technological skills, you want to nip them in the bud so that they can focus on what really matters: why you are the best person for the job they need to fill, and how soon you can get to work. Put simply, if a prospective hiring manager uses LinkedIn to learn about your work experience and is unable to find your profile, they will view this as a definitive and objective confirmation of their concern and move on to the next candidate.

I often advise younger candidates to share less on social media. With older candidates, however, I suggest the opposite: You want to share as much as you can about your background, so that your experience and qualifications stand out. This means creating your own Facebook and/ or LinkedIn accounts and updating them regularly. If you are not comfortable setting up the accounts, reach out for guidance. Your family and friends likely possess the basic skills necessary to get started. If not, for a relatively small sum of money, you can hire a professional to provide you with a basic account set-up.

Once you have established the accounts, start using them actively. On Facebook, be sure that you do not limit your connections to a handful of friends. Connect with people from all walks of life, to show that you are a vibrant professional candidate who leads a full life. (This will also help you with networking, an element we will discuss later.) Reach out to your children and grandchildren as initial connections; you will be surprised at how rapidly your reach will grow. If you are unsure whether prospective employers will appreciate some of your posts, adjust your setting so your account is private.

Along the same lines, maintain an active and frequent presence on LinkedIn, which is a professional networking website, unlike Facebook, which is more of a personal network. If you are not familiar with LinkedIn, there are many resources available to provide you with the basic skills you will need to optimize your profile and make the most of the job-search tools it offers. You might even want to look for a free or low-cost webinar so the benefit will be two-fold, providing you with some information about how to make the best use of your profile and also helping you to become more comfortable with online learning.

Once your social media pages are up and running, be sure to use them. Participate. Post. Engage. Social media interactions are a great way to alert a wide audience to the fact that you are not a passive job seeker looking to fill her time, but an active, aggressive job seeker looking to make a contribution and continue to grow and learn. Make sure your posts present a picture to prospective employers of the precise type of employee you will be once you find the right job opportunity.

DO NOT DELIVER BY CARRIER PIGEON

Once your online presence starts to materialize, and your cover letters and resume are ready to go, be sure to continue to remind any prospective hiring manager that you are comfortable with technology. This means, among other things, that if the company requires an online application, be sure to apply online. If a prospective employer asks you to upload a copy of your cover letter and resume, be sure to upload them as opposed to sending them by fax because you are not comfortable working with attachments. If you are not comfortable uploading these materials on your own, you can usually get assistance with these services at your local library or at your local copy store.

Once you have mastered the art of cover letter and resume writing, the next step is to start working on your interview skills. Playing to your audience and, more specifically, finding ways to incorporate the various themes we have discussed thus far, are covered next with Strategy #2.

POSTSCRIPT

COVERING THE BASES OF YOUR RESUME AND COVER LETTER

"A resume is a balance sheet without any liabilities."
—Robert Half

There are plenty of books devoted to the subject of how to write resumes and cover letters, so I will limit this discussion to the very basics, with some specific advice that relates to candidates of a certain age. Of course, rather than using a generic cover letter, you will want to tailor your letter to the position for which you are applying. Look to the specific job skills listed in the job posting and provide specific examples that clearly illustrate that you are the Cinderella fit. Remember to focus not only on what you have accomplished, but on how your accomplishments can benefit a prospective employer.

Once you have covered the basics, make sure your letter projects the sort of image discussed in this chapter. Present yourself as an active candidate with great enthusiasm and energy for tackling new projects. Rather than just focusing on your record for accomplishing the goals of your current position, focus on any accomplishments you actively sought out. Exhibit a consistent interest in learning by referring to any recent job-related relevant course you took or conferences you attended. Where practical, illustrate how you helped your current employer modernize some of its business practices. Showcase your technological skills as often, and in as many ways, as possible. If there are technological components of the position, be sure that your cover letter makes it clear you possess the necessary skills to excel in that component of the role.

In the ideal situation, the cover letter will be the first document that a prospective hiring manager reviews, followed by your resume (which should reinforce the vibrant image you have painted). However, some hiring managers forgo the cover letter and go straight to the resume. Not only that, but given how easy it is to share documents (thanks to technological advancements), you never know who else in the company will see your resume during the initial decision-making process. For this reason, make sure your resume is perfect both in style and substance, so that it stands out on its own and gets the appropriate level of review.

While one can argue that crafting a resume is subjective, there are, in fact, certain standards that employers look for. The most common type is a chronological resume, which generally starts with a professional summary at the top of the document, followed by a list of past employers (starting with the most recent). In contrast, a functional resume focuses more on the candidate's skills, listing those at the top, followed by a list of past employers (which is generally found at the bottom of the page). There are some pros and cons related to the use of each of these types of resumes, and some other variations do surface from time to time.

Regardless of which style you choose, be sure your resume is an appropriate marketing tool in the loyalty-free workplace. Frame your experience so that it meets the needs of a prospective employer (as opposed to meeting your own), while disavowing any notions that you are anything short of the Cinderella fit.

INFUSE YOUR RESUME WITH TECHNOLOGICAL REFERENCES

As with the cover letter, be sure your resume tells a prospective employer that you are comfortable with technology. Right at the top of your resume you want to include your e-mail address, website, Twitter handle, and the link to your LinkedIn profile. At a minimum, you need to have a professional sounding e-mail address. ("Foxygrandma@whateveryouremailserveris.com" is not the image you want to project, for reasons we have discussed.) If you went to a well-known school and still have access to that e-mail address, you should use that e-mail account (provided you check it regularly). You should also include a mobile number, which indicates your ability to accept a text from a prospective employer in the event that is how they elect to communicate.

As a general rule, your resume should be between one and two pages, and include only information that directly relates to the position for which you are applying. This means you do not want to provide what is known as a "career obituary," a resume that details work-related (and in some cases non-work related) experiences from decades ago. Yes, this means that you can likely remove the reference to the high school you attended and any group memberships from college, unless there is some specific reason why that information would be relevant to the vacant position. The same holds true for any leadership positions held decades ago. Presumably, if past leadership positions were beneficial, you used them as a springboard to more relevant and likely more senior leadership positions that will be of much greater interest to a hiring manager. You will want to use a current example of the development of the same or a similar skill.

Since most hiring managers want to know whether you possess relevant experience, they will want to see the dates you worked for certain employers. To meet this need, I would recommend including the most recent twenty years of work experience and the corresponding dates.

If you find yourself in a situation where some of the employers in your distant past are relevant to a particular position, you can add a section on your resume after you detail your more recent experience titled "Previous Positions Held," or "Prior Related Work Experience," and simply list those employers without providing further details. Because most employers look for recent experience, and because most are inclined to believe that skills developed years ago are less likely to be beneficial than skills developed in the recent past, it is best to focus on your most recent experience and target jobs that are most aligned with those skills.

If you find yourself in a situation in which you do not have the most updated skills, but you have taken a class or webinar to develop them, put that on your resume. This will show the hiring manager that you have the skills, while dissuading any perception that you no longer have a willingness to learn. If you are unable to complete the training prior to submitting your application, you can still list it on your resume along with the qualifier that you are "currently enrolled" in the class or that you are "in progress."

Finally, be sure to review your resume to be sure that it reflects the most current industry standards. Remove any terms that suggest you are an older candidate or a candidate that does not have current knowledge about industry trends. Where possible, substitute more "modern" terms for those that suggest that you might be behind the times, and remove skills that are not likely to be relevant. Few employers are looking for administrative assistants who have word processing skills or are able to use Dictaphones, nor are employers looking for technicians who can repair mimeograph machines.

Remember, too, that many online application systems are programmed to identify certain application keywords, just as recruiters often search LinkedIn profiles for certain keywords associated with qualified candidates. Be sure that you have those keywords on your resume. When applying for specific jobs, use the words used in the job description in your resume and cover letter where appropriate to increase the chances of producing a match. We will talk more about this later in detail.

STRATEGY #2

PLAY TO YOUR AUDIENCE

First things first. If it has been a while since you last went out on a job interview, you will want to brush up on your interview skills. This has nothing to do with your age, by the way—it is just common sense. Even the most successful business people, regardless of their age or industry, engage in some preparation before sitting down or logging on for an important meeting. How much or how little preparation you will need will depend upon your area of expertise and your comfort level with interviews in general. If you are used to speaking in front of people, you may feel more comfortable tackling the interview process, particularly once you become aware of the parameters discussed in this book. On the flip side, if you work in a job that is more isolated, and that does not necessarily require you to engage in one-on-one conversations in the workplace, you might want to seek out a professional who can provide some basic interview coaching.

Regardless of whether or not you hire a formal interview coach, you should be certain to engage in mock interviews with other working professionals who are willing to evaluate your performance. Many job candidates have found recording their mock interviews to be incredibly effective, since this allows them to see (or hear, if you only choose to record the audio) the image they are portraying and adjust their behavior based on those results. And as most smartphones or laptop computers have video cameras and/or audio recorders already built in, assuming you already have these devices, this is neither difficult nor expensive to do.

"I thought I was on the road to success,
but my GPS maps were out of date!"

If you are not inclined to invest in a traditional interview coach, at the very minimum you should practice interviewing with some colleagues, family members, or friends. Just be sure to invite at least a few working professionals who are younger than you. For one, this will provide you with a sense of the types of questions a younger hiring manager may pose, so you can prepare for the wide range of issues that may be discussed. In addition, you can ask the practice interviewer to be particularly aware of any statements you make, or conduct you engage in, that may feed into the negative stereotypes attributed to older candidates. (Not to sound ageist, but someone who is close to your age may not be as aware of these nuances as someone from a different generation.) If possible, include people who are familiar with the hiring process, particularly with regard to positions at the level for which you will be applying and in the industry in which you are looking for a job.

As you gear up for an interview, remember to implement the strategies we have discussed so far to any and all interactions with the prospective employer. This is important because the interview process is much more than the 45-minute conversation you may have in an office with the hiring manager. Every direct or indirect connection you make with people in the process provides a prospective employer with information as to whether you will be a match for the position. Now that you know that you have a good idea of the perceptions that you will have to overcome, everything you do should be geared toward stripping down those stereotypes.

> Sophie Gessler reaches out to candidate Logan Vesper, 58, to schedule an interview for a customer service representative. Sophie informs Logan that she has an early morning appointment and one later in the afternoon. Logan responds that she is not a morning person and would much prefer the afternoon appointment.

While it is true that Sophie is offering Logan two different interview times, which suggests either option is agreeable to the company, Logan wants to send a consistent message that she is an active and eager candidate with as much energy, if not more energy, than any other younger applicants. Remember, older candidates do not want to give off the impression they will be less than wide awake and eager to report to work each morning. Telling anyone involved in the process that you are not a morning person is inconsistent with the picture you want to paint.

If Logan is truly not a morning person and believes she will perform better in the afternoon, then by all means she should select that interview time. However, there is no need for her to provide an explanation for her desire for the later time slot, especially if the explanation has the potential to feed into the negative stereotypes related to the low energy level of older applicants.

LOOK AND FEEL THE PART

On interview day, it is critical that older candidates focus on the exhibition of this same heightened energy level. If you have to walk up a flight of stairs to get to the interview and are out of breath, take a minute to regain your composure before approaching the reception area. Be sure to eat before you go into an interview, to be properly hydrated, and refrain from smoking (or being in the vicinity of smokers) before your meeting. Do not discuss the fact that you are just getting over another cold because everyone on the subway was coughing on your way in. Remember, you want everyone to view you as a vibrant and healthy employee, not one who is likely to use their entire sick leave allotment.

Now a word about wardrobe: When interviewing for a job, you want to project an image of "today." This applies to not only understanding the state of the current marketplace, but what you wear. Not to suggest that all hiring managers are shallow, but you will have a difficult time convincing an employer that you are up to speed on the latest trends if you show up wearing a suit that you last wore twenty years ago.

It does not matter whether that suit still fits perfectly, or whether you happen to be in better physical condition than the person conducting the interview. Like everything else in life, fashions change. A bad choice in wardrobe can undo all the work you have done to prepare for the interview. For this reason, dress in a manner that fits the times and projects a youthful attitude, even if you get a sense that the company is not particularly concerned about whether or not your clothes reflect current fashion trends.

> "When my daughter's boyfriend was preparing for a job interview, he balked at having to dress up. 'It's a casual office,' he argued. 'Why should I show up in a suit and tie?' Our daughter, Heather, smiled and told him, 'You have to make the team before you get to wear the uniform.'"
>
> —Dorothy Davis

Does this mean you should dress like someone who is in their twenties? Of course not! All that will do is call attention to the fact that you are of a certain age. All I am suggesting is that your clothes and accessories be as current as the knowledge you bring to the position. The best way to convey that image is to dress in a manner so that no one notices or comments on your attire, but instead focuses on your qualifications. This usually means a navy, gray, or black suit, and a modern, neat haircut. But this might mean something different if you are applying for a job with a start-up that prides itself on allowing individuals to wear beach attire to work.

In addition, in your interview be sure to use every opportunity to address any other misconceptions about your age. For example, of course you will want to be sure your phone is turned off during the interview, but should you ever be in a position where you need to remove it from your bag, be sure you are holding one of the latest phones and not a flip phone that is in need of an upgrade. If you do have an older phone, be sure to keep it out of view. Be sure not to emphasize the fact that your family makes fun of you because you still have a landline. See Postscript: Overall Health and Well-Being for some further guidance on how to present your best self.

Regardless of when you last went out on an interview, remember that you are now interviewing for a job in the loyalty-free workplace. Like all other steps in this process, everything you say in the interview should be geared toward identifying what the employer wants and how you can supply that. Like any other new mindset, it may take a while to master. The best way to do so is to practice discussing some of the most common questions and topics that come up in an interview and gear your answers accordingly.

LET THE EMPLOYER COUNT THE WAYS YOU ARE THE BETTER FIT

> Hiring manager Vivian Evens asks job applicant Ellie Rasher, 55, why she is interested in working as the paralegal coordinator for her law firm. Ellie explains that she has worked as a paralegal for over twenty years and is ready for a new challenge that would enable her to develop her supervisory skills.

While Ellie's answer is perfectly legitimate, it speaks more to her needs, not to why Vivian should hire her over the dozens of other candidates who applied for the position. Similarly, it is not enough to tell the interviewer that you bring x number of years of experience to the table. Your job is to convince the interviewer of the benefit the employer can derive from those years of experience.

After working for thirty-five years for the same employer, accountant Rhett Daniels is laid off from his position that required him to prepare tax returns for hundreds of small business clients. Rhett applies for a position as an accountant for a new startup company and is offered this position.

If you are the hiring manager, the benefit of hiring Rhett is not that he has thirty-five years of experience, but that he prepared taxes during thirty-five different tax seasons, and, therefore, has dealt with a wide range of issues faced by a wide range of small businesses during that time span. That is a tangible, objective, and measurable indicator of his experience that differentiates him from other candidates. Even if there was another applicant in the running with thirty-five years of experience, if that person specialized in one particular area, she would not have the broad spectrum of knowledge that Rhett has to offer. He took inventory of his experiences and packaged it in a way that was of value to a prospective employer. This is the key to finding a job in today's work environment.

Going back to Ellie's example, if she were my client, I would suggest that she answer the "why are you interested in this job" question more or less like this:

While developing my paralegal skills, I have had numerous opportunities to streamline the way in which work is assigned, replacing the rotational assignment process with a new process by which paralegals who have worked on similar projects are given first priority for those assignments. This new system enabled our team to increase the efficiency of our operations by 12 percent. I am eager to find a new position that will offer more frequent and more formalized opportunities to identify areas of improvement and implement processes to achieve them.

For the most part, this response is much the same as Ellie's first reply, in that it states her desire to develop her leadership and supervisory skills. Why is it a better response? Because it presents Ellie as a problem solver who tangibly improved the bottom line of her previous employer. If Vivian believes that her firm could likewise benefit from Ellie's experience, Ellie will be in the best position to receive the offer.

Packaging your experience into measurable terms will do away with any stigma the interviewer may have about your number of years of experience.

> Paul Verano, 62, applies for a position as the labor relations director of a large manufacturing company. Paul drafts a cover letter in which he explains that he has close to three decades of experience negotiating and administering union contracts, which will enable him to hit the ground running in the new position. After reviewing his cover letter with a career coach, Paul revises his letter to explain that as an experienced labor relations professional, he has successfully negotiated more than two hundred labor contracts and has developed strong personal relationships with the nine major manufacturing unions with whom the company has contracts. Paul is invited to interview for the position.

In advising Paul, the career coach borrowed a page from Rhett's playbook, so to speak, by suggesting that he present his experience in terms of a meaningful number—how many contracts he has successfully negotiated—not what might be a meaningless number—how many years he has been doing it.

Put another way, we have all heard the old adage, "Age is just a number." From the point of view of the hiring manager, the same idea follows. Meaning, having nearly thirty years of experience is a nice number, but it says nothing about

> "Does he have 17 years of experience or one year of experience 17 times?"
> PAUL R. WIESENFELD

what Paul can do to benefit the manufacturing company. Not only that, but as we have seen before, "thirty years of experience" might suggest that Paul's skills are outdated, that he no longer has an interest in learning, or that he is not open to change. Now that Paul's revised approach resulted in a job interview, he needs to establish in the interview that he has a proven track record of results related to the work required for this new position. That will support his case that he is, in fact, the Cinderella fit.

CONSIDER THE SOURCE OF YOUR MEASURABLE RESULTS

Another source of objective support is what your prior supervisors think about your work. Any information you can provide an interviewer to bolster your qualifications will take you one step closer to receiving the job offer. Toward that end, besides making the case yourself, come to the interview prepared with a list of characteristics that describe you and your work ethic, as well as any documents you have to support these characterizations. If you have received strong performance reviews in the past, bring copies with you so that you can leave them with the interviewer. This can particularly help your cause if your performance reviews address some of the job tasks you have completed in the past and will be required to continue to perform in the position. On top of that, even if you bring your performance reviews to your interview and do not hand them over, by reviewing them you will very likely find some information that you could work into your interview to further your candidacy.

> Richard Walters, 66, interviews for a position as a marketing manager at a large insurance company. When asked to provide the three adjectives his prior supervisor would use to describe his work style, Richard replies, "Experienced, loyal, and creative."

Richard's answer describes an ideal marketing manager: namely, someone who not only has the necessary experience, but realizes that sometimes you have to utilize creative strategies to secure new business. In addition, Richard's adjectives are particularly effective because they highlight the benefits of being an older candidate (experienced), while also addressing a significant employer concern related to employee turnover: the reluctance of candidates to commit to the employer for an extensive period of time (loyalty). Questions such as these can be challenging to answer on the spot, and with limited time a candidate might provide a response that only addresses one of the concerns (the loyalty-free workplace) and not the other potential concern (age). By mapping out a strategy before the interview, Richard worked to address two potential concerns the interviewer might have had with his application.

USE THE ROAD MAP YOU HAVE BEEN GIVEN

Given how important it is to frame your qualifications around meeting the needs of the employer, is there a surefire way of anticipating exactly what those needs are? Short of having a crystal ball, the answer is no. But if you do your homework, and know where to look for the answers, once you sit down for the interview you will have already strategized how to present yourself in the best possible light.

For example, by the time you report to the interview, you should have a good idea of the employer's precise hiring needs by virtue of the job description. There it is, all spelled out for you, in writing. During the interview, assuming you have reviewed the job description closely, you can proactively look for opportunities to talk about the specific skills you have that relate to each aspect of the position.

In an ideal situation, you will have prepared a written document that you can use as a cheat sheet. On the left side, list each job requirement and qualification. On the right side, list not only which skill(s) of yours enables you to meet the requirement, but examples from your prior work experience that illustrate just that. Assuming you have gone over this list a number of times before the interview (both on your own and during your mock interview), you will have a number of ways to bring up these examples in the course of the conversation—all of which show, in quantifiable and measurable terms, how you can contribute to the company. This, in turn, will suggest to the company that it should not only hire you, but pay a premium price for your contribution.

HOW TO TALK ABOUT YOURSELF EFFECTIVELY

Preparing a list of talking points can also help you answer one of the first questions an interviewer may ask: "Tell us a little about yourself." Now, some of you may be thinking, "That is a pretty easy question. Why do I need a cheat sheet for that?" Because it can help you stay on point. After all, you have a limited amount of time to show the interviewer that you are the Cinderella fit. And your talking points will steer you away from making any sort of comment that might evoke some of the negative perceptions we have discussed related to older candidates.

Paige McGregor starts the interview of sales manager candidate Lewis Alvarez, 59, by asking him to tell her a little bit about himself. Lewis explains that he really enjoys traveling, and now that his children are out of the house, he is looking forward to making up for lost time.

On the one hand, Lewis' response is a perfectly legitimate response that, depending on the interviewer, might lead into a very pleasant exchange. On the other hand, the comment about traveling (and "making up for lost time") could be problematic for a number of reasons. First, traveling requires missing days of work. If you are a hiring manager, the last thing you want to hear or see on a resume is how much a candidate loves to travel, because that suggests the candidate will be using all of their vacation time. Of course, an employee has the right to use all of their allotted vacation time, and many supervisors will even encourage that. Even so, there are better ways to break the ice. After all, a job interview is a competition. You never want to say anything that might eliminate you from contention right off the bat.

In addition, upon hearing that Lewis' children are adults and on their own, the hiring manager might pigeonhole Lewis as a candidate who may be less motivated or less dedicated to his work than a younger candidate with three children who still need to have their college tuition paid. Yes, this is a stereotype that may not reflect Lewis' situation at all. For all we know, he may be a workaholic who thrives on the productivity of 60-hour work weeks. The point is, Lewis needs to present himself as precisely the sort of vibrant, committed, and eager employee the manager wishes to hire. He would have been better off saying:

> I love working in sales and sharing that enthusiasm with others. I have learned the importance of maintaining the morale of my sales teams and developed an incentive-based compensation system, which resulted in an 18 percent increase in sales over the past three years, and a 96 percent retention rate over the past five years. I achieved these results after having implemented just three of the five steps of my long-term plan for the company.

Here, Lewis took advantage of the opportunity to provide a specific and measurable example of what he accomplished in the past and the potential for him to achieve these same results for the prospective employer. Just as important, nothing in this response suggests that he is ready to retire or even thinking of retiring.

ILLUSTRATE THAT YOU ARE UP TO THE CHALLENGE

Another question that job interviewers like to ask is "Discuss a challenge you have overcome." While the question does not necessarily relate to your job or career, a savvy candidate will provide an example that is not only work-related, but which provides concrete evidence that she is, in fact, the perfect fit.

> Kaylee Halbert, 59, applies for a position as the general counsel of a major music label. During the interview, the hiring manager asks Kaylee to talk about a situation where she had to deal with a challenging personality. Kaylee says that she once had to have a conversation with a senior executive of a former employer who continued to tell inappropriate jokes during work retreats, resulting in a number of complaints.

Why is this a good answer? Because it illustrates Kaylee's capacity for dealing with difficult employees in an effective way. This is the sort of detail a prospective employer wants to hear, because it can also benefit them.

If you are interviewing for a position with supervisory responsibilities, give an example of how you managed a difficult employee. If it is a sales position, tell the story about how you took on a client that no one wanted to touch—and closed a deal with results far beyond the company's expectations. Whatever the job entails, make sure that your response provides specific, measurable, and narrowly tailored evidence of your qualifications and supports your application.

HOW TO DISCUSS YOUR STRENGTHS AND WEAKNESSES

> Prospective employer: What is your biggest weakness?
> Candidate: Honesty.
> Prospective employer: That's quite interesting. I have never
> thought that honesty was a weakness.
> Candidate: I don't give a @$#@ what you think.
> —Unknown

This is another common question that can pose pitfalls for job candidates of a certain age. Like everything else we have discussed so far, some answers are more effective than others:

> Harper O'Bryan, 51, applies for a position as the chief of staff for a national retail chain. When asked to discuss one of her weaknesses, Harper explains that she has found it difficult to identify candidates for mid-manager positions because, in her experience, most individuals who apply for these types of roles are either overqualified and underqualified.

Believe it or not, that was the applicant's answer. When asked to elaborate, Harper explained to me that she was being honest and that she did not want the employer to think that she was arrogant. Despite her successful track record, she did not believe that she was skilled at filling jobs at every level, and she wanted to illustrate she had been willing to reach out for assistance. While that is an admirable trait under some circumstances, that is not what a prospective employer wants to hear from a prospective chief of staff. In other words, they are looking for someone who *can* fill any job that needs to be filled, at any time. While it is true that many good leaders will reach out for assistance in making key decisions, their ability to make decisions is what makes them good leaders.

Remember, a job interviewer is looking for ways to eliminate you from contention. You need to make that task as difficult as possible. While

©Glasbergen
glasbergen.com

**"Leadership experience?
I have 13 people following me on Twitter!"**

honesty is always the best policy, in Harper's case it made the company believe that she was not the right candidate, when in fact she probably was.

Here is another tricky question: "Is there any reason why our company should not hire you?" Here again, your list of talking points will tell you how to navigate it—only in this case, you want to be sure that this weakness does *not* relate to any of the skills on the list.

> Angie Brady, 59, is among the finalists for a chief of staff position. When asked to explain one of her weaknesses, she explains that she spoils her grandchildren by taking them on bimonthly wilderness hiking trips.

Why is this a bad answer? Primarily because it has nothing to do with the job for which Angie is interviewing (which, depending on the interviewer, might eliminate her from the running on that basis alone). And even though this response does present the picture of Angie as a vibrant and active grandparent, it does not say whether she would be just as vibrant and active as an employee.

Now, perhaps the interviewer likes Angie as a candidate and does not hold that answer against her. He may reiterate the question, this time asking for a job-related weakness. If you are Angie, your best bet is to use a weakness that you may have had that you have since addressed.

> When asked to provide a job-related example of a weakness, Angie explains that she used to be less than 100 percent comfortable with public speaking. But because she had been required to give a number of presentations in her prior position, she took a public speaking class at the local community college and now has significantly improved those skills.

Here, Angie has identified a job-related weakness—since the chief of staff position will, at the very least, require her to engage in conversations with others (and, possibly, speak in public). However, by bringing up examples of how she has addressed that weakness, she discussed it in a way that accentuated her current level of skills, which would benefit the company if they hire her. In addition, by indicating that she took a class in public speaking, Angie also did away with any notion that she was no longer willing to develop her skills further or adapt to her new work environment.

ONCE YOU HAVE LEVELED THE PLAYING FIELD, TAKE IT UP A NOTCH

In each step of the job-search process, you want to show the hiring manager that you are on the same level as any younger applicants. Once you have done that, be prepared to discuss any qualifications you may have that set you apart from the other candidates. Why? Because all things being equal, a hiring manager might be inclined to extend an offer to a younger candidate, for any number of reasons. Therefore, even if you have the same skills as all of the other younger candidates, you will still need to show the employer what skills you possess that should tip the scale in your favor.

> Celeste Jacker, 61, applies for a position as a public health advisor. During the interview, the hiring manager asks Celeste to explain what sets her apart from other candidates. Knowing that one of the qualifications listed in the job description is exceptional writing skills, Celeste explains that she not only wrote three grant applications on behalf of her company (all of which resulted in funds for the company), but she is also the author of two novels.

Grant writing is a particular form of writing that requires certain skills to succeed. Besides illustrating her qualifications for the job that she is interviewing for, the grant writing example shows that Celeste brought value to her previous company (in the form of the monies awarded from each of the three grants). Not only does that distinguish her from other candidates, should the prospective employer hire Celeste, they might also benefit from her grant-writing abilities should they apply for a grant in the future. In addition, while writing two novels is not directly tied to the position, it does bolster the perception that she is a proficient writer, and it is also something that will distinguish Celeste from the rest of the pack.

OF COURSE YOU HAVE QUESTIONS— BE SURE TO ASK THE RIGHT ONES

As the interview winds down, you will likely be asked whether you have any questions for the prospective employer. This, again, is an opportunity for you to create the impression that you are the perfect fit. You will want to have a number of questions prepared that you can use to cement that impression on the mind of the employer, while alleviating any concern about your age or your ability to do the job. You can also use the opportunity to direct the conversation in a way that will provide you with an opportunity to share information with the employer that you think perfectly illustrates your fit but did not yet come up in your discussion.

Erika Waverly, 51, is reaching the end of her interview for a position as an insurance salesperson, and she has not been able to talk about the significant outreach she has done in her current job, which brought in more than twice the number of new clients her employer had expected. Remembering that the company stated on its website that its goal for the new year is to develop new products for specialized markets, she asks whether the person hired into the new position would be involved in that expansion. The interviewer says yes, the initiatives were company wide (which is something Erika surmised, based on her research). "I am excited to hear that," Erika replies. "I recently spearheaded a new policyholder drive with my current employer. I hope to have the opportunity to work on similar projects in a new position."

The point is that you should enter the interview with a list of your qualifications that you think make you the ideal fit for the position, and once you have completed the interview, you should feel confident that you have presented the prospective employer with all of the information they need to conclude that you are an ideal candidate and that you have done everything you could have to move forward in the process. To be sure of this result, job candidates should look for some type of confirmation that their confidence is not misguided and is a true reflection of how the interview transpired.

What is the best way to do that? By being proactive with the final question you pose. Inform the hiring manager that, based on what you have discussed, you are confident that you have the precise qualifications and skills to be the ideal candidate for the position. Then take it one step further by saying that if the employer does have any concerns, you would be happy to discuss them.

Is that being a little forward? Yes, and I realize that not everyone may be comfortable doing that. But consider this: If the employer does have a concern about your candidacy (and actually shares it with you), not only will this alert you to a situation that you might not have thought about, it will give you a golden opportunity to effectively address it.

Greg Schaffer, 52, interviews for a number of vice-president positions with large financial institutions. He often moves forward in the interview process, only to be eliminated in the final round of interviews. At the end of one final round, after stating his belief that he is the ideal candidate for the position, Greg asks the prospective employers if they have any concerns he has not addressed. The interviewer explains that while they believe he has a great range of substantive experience, he appears to lack experience with foreign clients, which is the market that the institution expects to penetrate in the long term. In response, Greg explains that, in fact, he does have experience with foreign clients, but did not highlight those qualifications because the institution's current client list includes only domestic clients.

The bad news? Even after providing this additional information, Greg did not get the job. The good news, however, is that now that Greg is aware of one of the reasons why he never received an offer, he can use this information to his advantage in future interviews by bringing up his experience with foreign clients when applicable (as well as including that expertise on his resume). Not only that, but if Greg's exposure to foreign clients was not as substantial as the prospective employer might have been looking for, Greg might consider looking for additional opportunities to work with foreign clients in his current role, so that he can update his resume accordingly.

The fact is that you cannot address or resolve an issue if you do not know it exists. Suppose that, in response to your question to the employer about whether they have any concerns about hiring you, the employer tells you they would like to hire you, but are fairly certain you would not be available on the date when they need you to start. If you have some flexibility in this regard, and you are in a position to start at an earlier date than you had anticipated, then you can inform the prospective employer that their concern is unwarranted and certainly should not be the basis for your elimination. And if a change is not possible (or not something you are willing to do), you can shift your focus to potential opportunities that have a real chance of resulting in a job offer.

Another reason why you want to learn as much as you can as to why you did not get the job is because, in many situations, the potential issue is age-related—but not in the sense of how old you are. Instead, it is quite possible that you may not have received an offer because the employer felt you were overqualified or overpaid and therefore declined to seriously consider you for the position. These are two considerations that older candidates often view as significant road blocks on their career paths, and how to get around them is what we will discuss next in Strategy #3.

POSTSCRIPT

OVERALL HEALTH AND WELL-BEING

As we age, we get tired! Even people in their thirties admit that they do not bounce back the morning after a late night of dancing and drinking as easily as they did when they were in their twenties. The older we get, the more energy it takes to get up each morning and to eagerly approach each work-day. That speaks to one of the most negative perceptions about older job candidates: Hiring managers believe that they will be more prone to illness, which can lead to excessive absences as well as increased healthcare costs.

Of course, this stereotype is unfair. There are just as many healthy and active older people as there are unhealthy and sedentary younger peo-ple. In fact, many people tend to adopt healthier habits as they age in response to a health scare and/or as a means of prolonging the aging process. However, given the realities of today's workplace, you will want to be sure that when a hiring manager views your application, and meets you in person, you present yourself as a vital, active candidate.

What steps can you take to work toward this goal? First, adopt a healthy lifestyle so it becomes apparent that you are committed to remaining energetic and active. The twenty pounds you put on while in college (when you were surrounded by junk food and alcohol) are not as notice-able in your twenties as they are in your forties and fifties. Show up to a job interview looking out of shape, and the prospective employer may wonder if you have the stamina required to maintain the hectic pace that most companies like to keep. Besides, since the issue about age is all about perception, by taking care of yourself physically you will you feel better mentally, which in turn will reflect how you present yourself.

Since you want to suggest that you are the picture of good health, avoid any comments or behaviors that suggest otherwise. For example, do not call a prospective employer to set up an interview when you are recovering from laryngitis or have a nagging cough—wait until you have your voice back. Along the same lines, do not mention any recent illnesses or hospital stays.

In addition, this may seem self-evident, but be sure that you are awake and attentive during the interview. If a twenty-year-old candidate asks an interviewer to repeat a question, it may not be noticed. If an older candidate makes the same request, however, a hiring manager may intentionally or even unintentionally see this as a reflection of your age (and, therefore, focus on someone younger).

As you move forward in the interview process, remember that employers collect information during all parts of the job search process, both formal and informal. That includes your phone and e-mail interactions with company employees while setting up the interview, as well as any lunches or dinners that you may be invited to attend as part of the recruitment process.

> Hiring manager Brooke Jasper invites one of the three finalists for a marketing manager position, Margaret Daventer, 53, out to lunch as a final step in the interview process. At the lunch, Margaret asks the waiter which of the available entrees have no added sugar because she is trying to maintain a healthy diet.

When out to lunch with a hiring manager, of course, you want to be sure not to ingest anything that puts your health at risk. However, to the extent possible, only select menu items that are best for you, without bringing attention to your illness. If you are concerned about added sugar, ask the waiter for a salad and some olive oil instead.

Although this may seem like common sense, many job candidates tend to relax when eating a meal with a potential coworker, and engage in behavior they might not otherwise exhibit in a formal interview. I have had lunch with candidates who inquire about the calorie count and sodium levels of certain entrees, as well as candidates who mention they avoid certain menu items because of their lactose intolerance! None of these discussions have a place in the interview process or even in any work-related meetings.

STRATEGY #3

TOO MUCH OF A GOOD THING IS NOT A GOOD THING

Can you ever *really* have too much of a good thing? Most of us have likely heard this before or even said it before. She loves decadent chocolate desserts, but after having three servings, leans back and proclaims, "too much of a good thing." When the lottery climbs to record heights, there is almost always a corresponding news story warning that the lucky winner may become a victim of the well-known curse, because, "you know what they say about too much of a good thing."

Quite often when my clients talk to me about their current jobs and their need to earn more money, they explain they are in a rut because of how much they love their jobs. I gently remind them that they should be working to earn the money they need to secure their futures, and if they love their jobs *too* much, they may become too committed and even put their future stream of income and the financial security of their family in danger.

Understanding that in the workplace too much may be too much is critical for older job candidates: The longer you are in the workforce, the more experience you will likely acquire. And while we may see an incredible value for every year of experience we get under our belts, prospective employers may see it differently.

Samantha Lever, 28, and Dan Harpaz, 57, both apply for a position as a sales manager at a national shoe company that manufactures high-end sneakers designed to be worn to formal affairs. Samantha has two years of experience covering fashion trends for a high-end fashion magazine. Dan worked at a family-owned shoe store for thirty-five years, explaining that during his tenure he sold back-to-school shoes to three generations of families. The two hiring managers declined to extend an offer to either candidate.

There could be a number of explanations as to why neither Samantha nor Dan were hired. It is possible that in Samantha's case, the hiring manager felt she was underqualified, because despite her knowledge of fashion trends, she has no experience selling shoes. In Dan's case, while he certainly had a lot of experience selling shoes, one could imagine that the hiring managers did not see how selling back-to-school shoes to the same customers year after year translated to an ability to sell high-end sneakers to a completely different demographic.

Then again, the hiring managers may have felt that Samantha was too young for the position, and Dan was too old. However, even if they actually said that, based on this set of facts alone, I would say that the rejection had less to do with either candidate's age, and more to do with the lack of a Cinderella fit.

Now, before you say "Yes, but I still think Dan was disqualified because of his age," remember that, in the loyalty-free workplace, the employer wants what the employer wants. Sometimes it really is as simple as that.

Say the hiring managers were looking for candidates with five years of experience selling shoes. On that criteria, you would think they would hire Dan. After all, he not only meets the minimum requirement, but brings a vast wealth of experience from an additional thirty years in shoe sales, from which the company can benefit. Yet, even if Dan presented himself in just that way, he still might not have gotten the job.

©Glasbergen
glasbergen.com

"We're looking for someone who isn't afraid
to fire people. You may be overqualified."

A DIABETIC DOES NOT WANT A CHOCOLATE BAR, REGARDLESS OF ITS DECADENCE

Why would a company reject a candidate who can offer more than what they are looking for? There really is truth to the statement that there is too much of a good thing in the realm of employment. Going back to the notion of perception, from a hiring manager's point of view "too much" likely has to do with everything Dan's experience represents: if Dan emphasizes the value of his thirty-five years of sales experience, he will likely expect a salary that is commensurate with that expertise. In other words, while they may appreciate Dan's level of experience and all that it offers, it is quite possible that they either cannot afford or simply do not want to offer a compensation package that is commensurate with Dan's experience. In this case, the extra years of experience, though valuable, are not valuable to them. This is something that candidates of a certain age must pay close attention to as they navigate the job search process.

In addition, in many cases when an employer decides what it wants, they become laser focused on achieving those precise specifications—not to mention the fact that there may be a significant disparity between how you define value and how the prospective employer sees it. And, even if you have something to offer that the employer might not have previously contemplated, in some cases it will be a challenge for you to convince an employer to modify its position related to what it is looking for in its new hire. With so many candidates competing for so few jobs, many hiring managers see eliminating candidates based on an objective qualification (such as "must have only five years of experience") as an efficient way to narrow the applicant pool, particularly if they can illustrate that past hires who had that precise level of experience have achieved success in their roles.

VALUE IS RELATIVE

You are likely familiar with the idiom that one man's trash is another man's treasure. Not to equate our experience with trash, but this idea does relate to the job search process. Allow me to explain.

I once attended a sports memorabilia estate sale with a group of friends who had eBay businesses through which they earned significant income. My entrepreneurial friends looked for heavily discounted items (usually a 90 percent discount) that they could purchase and then sell online (at 50 percent off the list price). From their point of view, that's a win-win: They make a profit off their original investment, while also providing an item that a buyer might not otherwise find at a discount.

At one sale, while my friends were clamoring for a particular hockey jersey and signed pair of sneakers, I stumbled on a box of women's clothes. Inside that box was a nearly new pair of Gucci shoes, which I purchased at 90 percent off the department store price and still have as part of my wardrobe.

People and things derive their value from those who are there to see them. To a roomful of sports memorabilia collectors, a pair of Gucci loafers has little, if any, value. But had those same shoes been on display in a second-hand clothing store, they would have gone for a lot more than what I paid for them. Similarly, job seekers must think creatively yet strategically when targeting appropriate employers for job opportunities. After all, value is in the eye of the beholder. What might be valuable to one person might have little, if any, value to another.

> Work–life balance expert Brenda Flukes, 53, is eager to apply for the vice-president position in the work–life balance department of a large computer manufacturing company. Brenda explains that she is reaching out to a number of people at the company to discuss the vacancy. Her primary goal is to arrange for an informational meeting with the CFO, the brother-in-law of an old college friend.

Given that Brenda has a personal connection with the CFO, I applauded her for "reaching for the top" to ensure that her resume is appropriately reviewed. At the same time, I suggested that approaching someone who held a different role at the company might yield a better result.

A CFO is concerned about the company's bottom line. While Brenda's extensive track record of creating and implementing work–life balance programs has the potential to be incredibly valuable to a company looking to invest in such programs (healthier employees mean a decrease in sick day use, which, in turn, could result in a significant increase in productivity levels), the CFO would likely see the costs involved (installing a gym in the office, offering additional healthy options in the lunchroom, and hiring a part-time nurse to staff a healthcare clinic) as expensive additions to the budget that he has to balance. An employee at a lower level might be more receptive to her ideas and, therefore, be more likely to help her get an interview (and possibly a job offer).

Similarly, and as we saw in the example with Dan, you may have thirty-five years of experience in the workplace, but that experience will be of no value to an employer who either does not need that level of experience or cannot afford it. This point is critical to understand, especially if you feel that you are not being considered for certain positions because you are overqualified.

Landing a job in today's workplace comes down to two things: (1) painting a clear picture of the value you will bring to a company, and (2) presenting that picture to the person who will most likely appreciate that value—the hiring manager. To achieve those goals effectively, it helps to understand how a hiring manager will, at least initially, assess your qualifications for a position.

PERSPECTIVE OF A HIRING MANAGER

Suppose you have fifteen years of experience and apply for a position that requires five years of experience. If you are currently employed, this may suggest to a hiring manager that you are not satisfied with your current position. In which case, the hiring manager might wonder if you are a difficult employee, have trouble getting along with others, or whether there is a problem with your overall work product. If you have been in the same position for fifteen years and have never been promoted, the hiring manager might also wonder whether you have reached your peak performance, or whether you are skilled enough to continue to remain employed, but *not* skilled enough to advance.

If you are not employed at the moment, the hiring manager might take that to mean that you are so desperate for work, you are looking for a job—any job—just to make ends meet until you can find a position in line with your skills.

Of course, it is possible that none of these situations apply to you. After all, there are plenty of reasons a candidate of any age might apply for a job for which they are overqualified. You may have a "Boss from Hell," or be in a toxic workplace environment or culture where you simply cannot thrive. Or you may be tired of the long commute and are willing to consider a job for which you are overqualified because the office is five minutes away from your home.

Once again, it is a matter of perception. A hiring manager is charged with filling a position with the best candidate possible. If you are applying for a position for which you are overqualified, the manager may very well believe that you are applying for a new job just to get out of your current job, or that you see this job as an interim position as you continue to job search. And under these circumstances, it actually makes good business sense not to consider you at all. Fair or not, since this is a common misconception and often a motivating factor that eliminates older candidates from consideration, it is a potential concern you will need to address.

THE PERSPECTIVE OF A JOB CANDIDATE

Now let us look at it from your point of view. If you are like most job searchers, you likely start the process by focusing on positions that match your level of experience.

> Ryan Cornelia, 52, comes across a job posting for communications director for a national public relations agency. The position seeks a candidate with ten years of experience. Because Ryan has twenty-five years of experience, he decides not to pursue the opportunity.

In theory, Ryan's response is the best strategic response, given the realities of the loyalty-free workplace. Yet you would be surprised at how many people actually target these positions because, even though they have far more experience than the position requires, they nonetheless believe that they are addressing the needs of employers. This is especially true if they have already sent out dozens of cover letters and resumes, only to be told they were "not good enough" or "not qualified" for the position. So if you have ten years of experience and are told you are not qualified for those positions, you decide you will have a much better chance at landing a job that requires eight, six, or even four years of experience. So what candidates do is cast a wider net by targeting jobs for which they know they *are* qualified—at least on paper.

This approach poses a problem. If a hiring manager wants to hire someone with ten years of experience, a candidate with twenty years of experience is just as unqualified as one with five years of experience. In the world of the Cinderella fit, that candidate with twenty years of experience has ten years more experience than the company wants or needs.

Yes, you say, but wouldn't the hiring manager see the wisdom of hiring someone like me? With my additional experience, I could do the job with my eyes closed. Perhaps you could, except that hiring

> "I'm not 54, I'm 18 with 36 years of experience."
> UNKNOWN

managers are not necessarily looking for candidates who can perform the job tasks with their eyes closed. Instead they may be assessing the likelihood that the hired candidates will continue to work for the company for the long term, especially in the loyalty-free workplace, for reasons we have already discussed. Therefore, this is something you will need to address.

And something to keep in mind is that the more years of experience you have under your belt, the more jobs you will see that require far less experience that what you have acquired. Therefore, if you do decide to seek positions for which you are overqualified, you must somehow offset whatever concerns the hiring manager may have about considering you as a candidate, which includes the managerial concern that you will continue to look for a new opportunity even if you are offered and accept a position with their company. The best way to do this is by both providing a plausible explanation for why you have applied for the job for which you are overqualified and illustrating that you are, in fact, seeking a long-term commitment.

WHAT WORKS FOR AGE ALSO WORKS FOR EXPERIENCE

How do you counter a hiring manager's perceptions that you may be overqualified? By applying some of the same strategies we have discussed related to the perceptions of age.

> Celeste Vegar, 51, is a patient care representative who has worked for the same assisted living company for fifteen years. During her time with the company, she was promoted fairly consistently, working her way up from a volunteer to a team leader. Celeste applies for a position that requires three to five years of experience in patient care, after the facility announces it is moving to a different state in order to take advantage of a new tax credit—a move that has been widely reported in the news. The hiring manager learns of the reason Celeste is applying for the position after a former colleague, who was Celeste's college roommate, sends him an e-mail alerting him to the application and vouching for her qualifications. The hiring manager invites her to interview.

Because the prospective employer knows why Celeste is applying for a position for which she is overqualified, Celeste not only gets in front of the issue, but quickly does away with it so that the focus becomes why she is the best fit for the position (which is how it should be). If you happen to find yourself in front a hiring manager before an explanation is conveyed, you could achieve this same result by starting your conversation by telling the manager, "I am interested in this position because I want to take my career in a new direction," "This is a great opportunity for me because I want to decrease my commuting time," or "I am eager to shift the focus of my career, which is why I am pursuing a more behind-the-scenes role in my industry."

CONVINCE THEM OF YOUR COMMITMENT

That said, even after you have allayed their concerns, there is no guarantee that you or Celeste or any overqualified candidate will be offered the position. There are other hurdles you will have to clear related to perception.

Remember, a hiring manager invests time, money, and other resources into identifying the best candidate for a position and then integrating them into the workplace. She is not likely to hire you if she thinks you will only stay with them until you find something better (in which case, she would have to start the hiring process all over again). Instead, prospective employers want candidates who are willing to commit to them for a few years. (In other words, they want someone who will stay in place, and not see the job as a placeholder.)

In addition, a hiring manager might also think that an overqualified applicant will consider some of the tasks associated with the position to be "beneath them." This touches on the concern we discussed earlier with regard to older candidates in general. If you happen to be in a supervisory position, one subtle way to address this concern is to complete some of the tasks that you might otherwise assign to others and list them on your resume. That way, a prospective hiring manager will see that continuing to perform those tasks will not be an issue, and that you are not so far removed from those responsibilities as the manager may have previously thought.

Then again, even if you take these steps, there is no guarantee that a hiring manager will bring you in for an interview. Why? Going back to our experienced shoe salesman Dan, this is because they will likely think your salary demands are beyond what they can afford to pay. For this reason, older candidates must also have a strategy in place when it comes to salary demands.

EXPERIENCE IS GOOD, BUT A TRACK RECORD IS BETTER

A common myth among older job seekers is the belief that their years of experience, in and of itself, will guarantee a certain level of compensation. This is, simply put, not true—if it was, then all employees who worked in a particular field for *x* number of years in a particular role would earn the same level of compensation. The reality is that a number of variables go into determining salary.

> Lily Norwood, 51, worked as a membership account executive for a national gym chain for close to three decades. She applies for a new position at a competing gym, noting her long-term service in her cover letter as a characteristic that distinguishes her from other job applicants. The hiring manager learns from a personal connection who works at the same gym that while Lily's sales numbers were consistent, they were also mediocre.

Remember, in the loyalty-free workplace, successful job candidates must present their qualifications in a way that meets the needs of the employer. If the competing gym is looking for a sales executive who can double their membership over the next year, an applicant with fewer years on the job, but a much stronger track record, would probably bring more value to the company than Lily, despite her extensive experience.

Not only that, but some hiring managers believe that the longer a candidate has worked in a particular role, the less value he can bring to the company. This is the basic idea espoused by Dr. Laurence J. Peter in his 1969 best-selling book, *The Peter Principle*. According to this theory, employees continue to be promoted as long as they excel at their job responsibilities; once they reach a level of incompetence, however, they remain in a position. As Dr. Peter put it, "the cream rises until it sours."

Am I in any way suggesting that this idea applies to you? Not at all, but what I am doing is giving you a window into the mind of a hiring manager. Since many hiring managers still believe in the *Peter Principle*, you must present your qualifications in a way that shows the hiring manager the true value of your experience, instead of assuming this will occur on its own.

AUTOPILOT COMPENSATION

Another common misconception among job candidates of a certain age is that a hiring manager will automatically offer a compensation package that is a certain percentage or dollar amount above their current earnings. This, also, is simply not true. Years of experience is just one of a number of factors that goes into the determination of a compensation package.

> Bob Everell, 54, has taught English at the same liberal arts college for twenty-five years. Each year, he received annual salary increases. After applying for a position as a full-time faculty member at another university, Bob tells the hiring manager that he expects to earn at least 10 percent more than he earned at his prior position.

Here again, more years does not necessarily mean more money. For all we know, Bob received a raise every year because his uncle was the president of the institution. Perhaps Bob was paid a higher hourly rate because he took on a heavier course load than any other teacher, or agreed to serve as the faculty advisor for certain student groups. From the hiring manager's point of view, the value of a position is derived from the position itself as opposed to other circumstances that may or may not be relevant to the position for which the candidate is applying.

YOU ARE A TRUE BARGAIN

Now, what if you find yourself interested in a position that offers a salary that is less than the market value for someone with your level of experience? If you are like most people in this scenario, you are probably either: (1) currently earning substantially less than the market value of your work, in which case what the employer sees as a pay cut is, to you, actually a salary increase; (2) willing to accept a pay cut, for whatever reason; or (3) plan to suggest that the prospective employer upgrade the position to find the ideal candidate (meaning you). Whichever situation applies, you need to get in front of the hiring manager in order to state your case. Without this personal interaction, the company will likely conclude that it cannot afford your services, or is uninterested in offering a salary commensurate with your experience, and therefore will not give your application any meaningful consideration.

> Emily Waffler, 61, is an event planner with more than thirty years of experience. She has only worked for two different employers, both of which were charitable institutions, and neither of which were willing to offer her a salary increase of more than 10 percent. Because of this situation, Emily earns significantly less than the market rate for someone with her level of experience. She applies for a senior position at a hotel chain. The job calls for someone with only fifteen years experience, but offers a salary that is well in excess of what she is currently earning.

In this case, Emily should make sure the hiring manager knows that the proposed salary will actually mean more money for her, thus alleviating any concerns the company may have as to why she would be willing to take a new job that requires less experience.

WILLING TO TAKE A PAY CUT

Moving on to the second scenario, since our career trajectories represent a number of hills, it is quite possible that there will be times when it makes sense for you to make a lateral move or even accept a salary reduction as a way to advance. Perhaps you work in a very specialized field with very few jobs and little movement within the industry. Or you may find yourself at a point where you want a fresh start in a new career in a new industry or a new geographic location where you know that maintaining your current level of compensation is not an attainable goal. Or you may find yourself in a dire situation, such as an eviction or the lapse of your medical benefits, that requires that you get a job—any job—as soon as possible. Or perhaps you are in the complete opposite position, where earning money is a secondary consideration, and therefore you are willing to work for less money in exchange for some work–life balance or more control over your schedule.

All of these are legitimate reasons for pursuing a position that offers a salary that is less than what you currently earn. The key to getting the offer under these circumstances is to be sure that you have the opportunity to let the hiring manager or recruiter know the reason you are prepared to accept this reduction—only then will they seriously consider you for the position. If you are able to meet face to face, you can state your case strategically and ease their apprehension. How do you do that? In some cases, all it takes is a simple "You may be wondering why I would be willing to consider a salary that represents a salary reduction. I am interested because, at this point in my career, I am fortunate enough to be in a position where the salary is a secondary consideration." This will go a long way in easing the employer's concerns because it provides a plausible explanation for your willingness to accept reduced compensation that is not detrimental to the employer's interests.

I often recommend raising the issue right away—get the elephant out of the room so that the rest of the conversation focuses on your qualifications. If you are not comfortable doing that, just be prepared to talk about it when the employer inevitably asks.

> Shelley Winters, 53, interviews for a position as a regional sales manager. The hiring manager explains that he is impressed with her qualifications, but is concerned about her salary expectations. He asks about her current salary.

In an ideal situation, Shelly should avoid providing her specific salary. Why? The greater the pay disparity between Shelly's demands and the budgeted compensation for the position, the greater the concern the prospective employer may have. Shelly may be inclined to throw out a low number in order to ensure that this gap is sufficiently narrowed, but then she may be leaving money on the table if the company actually had planned on offering a salary of a few thousand dollars more than the reduced number Shelly proposed. A more strategic answer, assuming she knows the salary range for the position, is for Shelly to say that she is "aware of the range and is comfortable with a figure within it."

Now, what if the employer presses you for an exact salary figure. Do you dodge the question? Even if you would rather withhold that information, I would recommend giving a figure, only because not answering that question could hurt your chances of landing the position. For one, an employer might wonder how you would conduct yourself in workplace situations when you might not want to fully disclose the requested information. Furthermore, unless you give the employer some idea of what you want, you will put them in a position of having to guess what you want—which might ultimately result in a waste of their time in the event an agreement cannot be reached.

> Shelley responds that she is comfortable with the posted salary range, which is $60,000–$70,000, but the hiring manager repeats his request for information about her current compensation. Shelley explains that she currently earns $85,000, but she is flexible and willing to discuss a salary that is within the posted range. She goes on to explain that she is looking for improvements in her total compensation, and views that as an all-inclusive number that includes medical and retirement benefits, vacation pay, and a desirable work schedule.

By telling the employer that she sees her job as more than just the numbers on her paycheck, Shelley indicates that she would be committed to the position in the event she was hired, while addressing the salary issue. That should eliminate any concern with regard to money.

MAKE A PITCH FOR AN UPGRADE

Now, what if Shelly was interested in the position, but the salary is not to her liking? In presenting herself to the prospective employer, she might float the idea that the additional value she would bring to the company warrants an enhanced compensation package. If the company agrees that it is in their best interest to hire her (and that is a big if, especially in today's workplace climate), they might also be willing to meet or at least more closely approach her salary demand.

Suppose you are in the market for a moderately priced car. You drop by the dealership and look at the row of cars that line the back end of the lot. Suddenly a salesman comes over and starts to talking about the benefits of owning a Lamborghini. Depending on how flexible your budget is, you might consider the possibility of spending more than you anticipated, or you might say, "No, thanks," and commit to staying within your means. The point is, you probably would have never even contemplated purchasing a more expensive car until the salesperson brought it to your attention.

Prospective employers are no different than people who buy cars. Sometimes they may be willing to "upgrade" by hiring someone who is more senior than previously anticipated, at a salary that is higher than they had anticipated paying. The only way you can know for sure is to make your best pitch. See if the employer might have the budget to offer a higher salary, then convince them that it is in their best interest to offer that extra budget to you. When you do, however, just remember that the employer is likely not the only one who establishes the budget for a particular position.

Consider a convenience store that sells milk and eggs. While it is true that the store's owner has the sole discretion to set price the price for eggs, the price may be impacted by a number of factors over which the owner may not have control. For example, if there is a shortage of eggs and the suppliers increase their prices by 30 percent, the owner may have no choice but to increase the price (particularly if the current selling price is not at least 30 percent more than what the owner paid). Similarly, if the owner prices the eggs at an exorbitant price and the eggs do not sell, the owner may be forced to reduce the price or risk the eggs expiring before being sold. If the owner is faced with an unexpected bill (such as the need to immediately replace a broken boiler), he may be forced to reduce prices temporarily to increase the store's cash flow.

This basic rule of the marketplace also applies to the workplace. Any number of forces may compel the employer to reevaluate its initial decision related to compensation

> Ian Reynolds, 52, a financial analyst at a brokerage firm, learns about a vacancy for a senior analyst position with another company. The position seeks a candidate with ten years of experience with a potential salary range of $125,000–$135,000, depending upon experience. Because Ian currently earns $160,000 and has twenty-five years of experience, he does not pursue the opportunity. Three months later, Ian learns that the position has been filled through an announcement in a trade magazine; three months after that, he reads a similar announcement that there is another new person filling the role. Not only that, one year later, he comes across the same job vacancy. This time, Ian applies for the position.

In this case, Ian likely made the right decision not to pursue the position initially. However, once the position had been posted and filled a number of times (most likely with candidates who fit within the advertised parameters), he felt that the company might be receptive to considering his application, since more than a year has passed since the company first posted the opening and they still had not found the perfect fit. This happens a lot in the workplace. Many employers will test the market by setting a budget for a position, only to adjust their settings if they find that their original budget was not enough to attract and retain the right candidate. This gives Ian a slight advantage, in that he might be able to convince the employer that filling the position with the right candidate is more important than staying within its budget.

YOU GET WHAT YOU PAY FOR

Granted, getting an employer to adjust its needs is as easy as herding cats. This is especially true if the employer happens to be strapped for cash, or is flooded with resumes for most vacancies. That said, there are some strategies you can use to get the result you want.

Assuming Ian is able to meet with the hiring manager, he will likely be told that his salary is "well in excess of what we have budgeted for the junior position." To turn that around, Ian must convince the company that they have got it wrong:

> "If you think hiring a professional is expensive, try hiring an amateur."
> UNKNOWN

It is not that they cannot afford to hire him, but that they cannot afford *not* to hire him.

> At a meeting with the hiring manager, Ian explains that he brings a unique perspective to the position, because he has a number of long-term, stable relationships with a number of clients—far more than what a candidate with only ten years experience would have.

The reality is that with age comes wisdom, which includes years of work experience and long-term relationships that have the potential to significantly benefit a prospective employer. By showing this prospective employer, in objective, measurable terms, that the employer will get what the employer pays for (i.e., his extensive experience with a number of clients), Ian presents a credible case for the compensation he is demanding.

Presenting objective evidence to support your salary demand will be critical. It is one thing to say that your experience justifies a six-figure salary. It is quite another if you are able to show that your salary demands are based on an analysis of what other people working in comparable positions earn.

> At the meeting, Ian explains that the average salary for people in his position is about $175,000, which is consistent with the compensation he expects to earn in his next role. He explains that this figure is consistent with the extensive salary research he did related to salaries offered by the company's competitors for similar positions. In addition, he explains that while he did find a handful of senior analysts who earn compensation in the range of $165,000, those directors do not work in major cities, where this position is located.

Here, Ian is providing specific, objective evidence to support his salary requests, providing the hiring manager with facts he can use to support a request for an increased budget for the position.

> "The bitterness of poor quality remains long after the sweetness of low price is forgotten."
> BENJAMIN FRANKLIN

STATE YOUR CASE WITH A PERIOD, NOT A QUESTION MARK

This may go without saying, but once you have developed your strategy and gathered the evidence to support it, execute your plan in a respectful but bold manner. This means making your salary demands firmly and with a period, not a question mark (as if you are asking the prospective employer whether they view the situation as you do). Even if they complain or seem unable or unwilling to meet your demand, be confident that you are worth every penny of what you asked. Do not apologize. Instead, do your best to convince them of your worth by showing the value you will bring.

In the ideal situation, Ian convinces the hiring manager that it is in the company's best interest to increase the budget for the position and extend an offer. It is also possible, however, that the hiring manager may agree that Ian is worth the extra compensation, but cannot afford to pay him due to budget constraints. If that is the case, there are a number of ways in which Ian and the company can work together to devise an agreeable compensation structure. For example, in some cases, a company's budget for a position is tied to a specific budget line. By dividing the payment in a different way (such as across two departments), the company may be in a position to attribute a portion of Ian's salary to a different budget line to bridge the gap that is necessary to reach an agreement.

What if the company simply does not have the money in its budget to pay Ian what he wants? Ian could ask for the difference between the salary the company is offering and the salary he expects to earn in a lump sum payment, rather than as part of his salary base. That would be a win-win: Ian maintains a significant portion of his salary, while saving the company some money, since future increases could be added to Ian's base (not including this bonus payment).

Another possibility: Ian could propose that the amount of money that separates the two parties be tied to Ian's performance. That way, if he brings in a certain amount of business, he would be entitled to the additional payment. This could be an effective compromise, because Ian can justify the payment by showing that his years of experience will enable him to bring in more new business than a younger candidate would bring.

Depending upon whether the hiring manager has the authority and the willingness to explore potential options, Ian might also suggest that the company slightly modify the position in order to justify the enhanced compensation. For example, suppose that when Ian applied for the financial analyst position, he noticed a number of other vacant positions that included supervisory responsibilities. Suppose also that the financial analyst position is not a supervisory role. To bridge the salary gap, Ian could propose that the company lift the supervisory responsibilities from one of the other vacant positions and make them part of the analyst role (along with an additional $20,000 in salary to reflect the compensation associated with these added duties). To keep everything within budget, the company could then reduce the salary of that other vacant position to reflect this change.

While this arrangement may not have been what the company originally had in mind, assuming that the hiring manager has the authority to "spend" the salary dollars in any manner he sees fit, this does provide a workable solution that meets the needs of both parties. See Postscript: Help the Hiring Manager Count the Ways for specific guidance on how to make a pitch for an upgrade.

KNOW WHEN TO HOLD 'EM, KNOW WHEN TO FOLD 'EM

Despite floating all of these possible solutions, Ian may still find that the hiring manager is either unwilling or unable to meet his salary demands. The reality is that even if the hiring manager recognizes the value of his experience and wants to hire him, because budgets are often set months in advance (usually in line with a company's fiscal year), he may not be able to adjust the budget until the start of the next fiscal year. In which case, Ian has to decide whether he is willing to walk away from the vacant position or accept a pay cut in exchange for a chance on a new opportunity.

Does this mean that the whole exchange was a waste of time? No. Because the hiring manager was at least willing to explore these options, this tells Ian two things: (1) The prospective employer sees value in what Ian can bring to the table, and (2) the very nature of the exchange gives Ian a good idea of what it might be like to work with the hiring manager and for the company in particular.

After going through this exercise, however, Ian should not assume that the company will be prepared to extend him an offer—even at a salary that is significantly below Ian's initial demand. Remember, most employers seek candidates who will commit to them for the long term. From what we know about the conversations between Ian and the manager up to this point, even if Ian accepted the lower salary, it would not fully satisfy him (and, therefore, he might use the offer as leverage for a more lucrative position in the future). For this reason, Ian must also assure the company that he would still do the work, even at a lesser salary.

As frustrating as it may seem, even if you do everything it takes to overcome the various hurdles facing candidates of a certain age applying for jobs for which they are overqualified, you are still facing an uphill battle with few guarantees.

IF YOU FIND IT IS MORE TROUBLE THAN IT IS WORTH, AVOID IT

There is, of course, one other way around this entire situation: You can simply avoid applying for these positions altogether and instead focus on jobs that match your level of work experience and that are in your current salary range. If you have fifteen years of experience, avoid applying for positions that seek five years of experience and you will not find yourself in the position of having to decide whether you should take a pay cut.

Remember, one of your biggest assets as an older candidate is that you do have experience, both in terms of the substance of your work and navigating the workplace in general. To the extent this is actually an advantage, I encourage you to use it.

Do not lose sight of the fact that the purpose of a job—any job—should be to earn increasing levels of compensation from year to year. Although in today's workplace this is no longer a guarantee, you will greatly increase the chances of this happening if you search for positions at your current level or at a higher level. Further, in the loyalty-free workplace, you will have better success of landing an offer if the job is aligned with your level of experience: Remember, employers want what employers want. Not only that, but because you have been able to land a job at your level of experience before, chances are you will be able to find a job at that level again. So, based on all of these workplace realities, the best strategy is usually to focus on those positions that are most closely aligned to your current level of expertise.

That said, each situation is different, and it is ultimately up to you to decide whether it is worth the time and effort to pursue a position for which you may be deemed overqualified and overpaid. If you do decide to go this route, then you will want to be sure to do all of the things

> "First you are young;
> Then you are middle-aged;
> Then you are old;
> Then you are wonderful."
> LADY DIANA COOPER

necessary to place yourself in the best position to obtain the desired results. As we have seen in many examples from this chapter, one of the keys to your success is to secure face time with the hiring manager so that you can make your best case for why you should get the job. But there is no guarantee that you will ever see the hiring manager, especially for jobs for which you are overqualified.

The good news is that there are some very specific strategies that you can use to increase your chances of securing that important face time, and specific ways to identify and hone in on your target audience are up next in Strategy #4.

POSTSCRIPT

HELP THE HIRING MANAGER COUNT THE WAYS

To achieve optimal results if you find yourself in Ian's situation, you need to (1) persuade the perspective employer that you are worth the value you demand, while (2) gently leading them to conclude that their expectations are not realistic. This, of course, can be challenging. Just as most candidates generally do research about a company before applying and interviewing for a position, employers also research the market trends related to the vacant position. The salary range for the position was likely based on a lot of thought, and is related to what comparable employees at the company and in the industry earn. You should remain aware of this and expect that the prospective employer will likely explain why its initial budget is a fair compensation structure. You, in turn, must be ready to provide evidence to support your position that this is not the case.

When approaching any negotiation, knowledge is power. Come to the table with specific numbers and objective evidence that suggests the salary you want is based on reality and reflective of your potential contribution. You will rely on your proven track record of results, which the other, more junior applicants will not possess. Provide salary information based on the earnings of colleagues and other people in your network who work in comparable positions. If you cannot find that information through people in your network, there are a number of great free resources at your disposal.

Start by doing a few basic searches on the most popular job boards in your industry. That will show you the trends in hiring and whether your salary demands are in line with them. If you are working with a recruiter, use information that has been presented to you for similar positions as further guidance. *Payscale.com*, *Salary.com*, *SalaryList.com*, and *Glassdoor.com* are free resources that provide a wide range of resources you can use to gather the information. Simply enter the specific information about the position you are searching, and the website will create a report that includes a wealth of compensation-related information that you can use.

The key is to provide a prospective employer with specific, objective, and verifiable salary information that will compel them to consider reviewing their current position as to the appropriate compensation level for the vacancy.

STRATEGY #4

IDENTIFY YOUR TARGET
BEFORE YOU SHOOT

Many older candidates tell me that one significant obstacle that continues to impede their job search is that there are simply no vacant jobs for them to fill. Consequently, some candidates throw their arms in the air and essentially give up.

> Ella Bayonne, 56, is a criminal defense attorney with decades of litigation experience. She meets with a career coach about her inability to secure a new position after the law firm where she worked downsized and eliminated 10 percent of its workforce. Ella explains that she has updated her skills, updated her resume, and drafted a number of model cover letters to ensure they paint a picture of a vibrant candidate. However, she does not know if her age will impact her ability to find a position because she rarely finds any vacant positions that match her qualifications and, therefore, rarely applies for any positions.

The problem with Ella's approach is clear: unless she pursues job opportunities she will never find one. But the good news for Ella is that there are jobs. Companies grow their existing businesses and companies create new businesses. Employees move and employees move on. Employees go on medical leave and employees go on personal leave. Employees retire and employees pass away.

> "You can't hit a target if you do not know what it is."
> TONY ROBBINS

And, there is more good news for Ella (or anyone else, for that matter). As of the time this book went to press, there are more than 4 million open jobs in the United States. And, if you are open to jobs outside of the United States, the number of vacancies is much higher. This is great for Ella because she only has to find *one*, and odds are there is more than one that is a match for her qualifications. And, even more good news: Since Ella has worked before, that means she has found a job before, so there is no doubt she can do that again.

The strategies we have discussed this far will help you circumvent the challenges that have previously stood in your way and greatly increase your chances of getting a job offer. But, of course, you will never see the benefits of these strategies unless you know how to find the opportunities in the first place. And if, like Ella, you are looking for opportunities and not finding any, then you need to modify your approach.

AVOID BEING A SPEEDING BULLET WITHOUT A TARGET

Most job seekers spend a significant amount of their time tapping familiar sources for vacancies, such as online job boards, newspaper and trade publications, and their alumni associations. While these are all great sources and should not be overlooked, they showcase a wide range of jobs to a wide range of people. As a result, you will often face significant competition for any posted position. Not only that, but chances are that the positions are not perfectly aligned with your particular experience and you will be spending a lot of time trying to mold your qualifications to fit the vacancies. Further, because these job postings are not usually updated in real time, by the time you submit your application, the position may have already been filled or, at a minimum, the first batch of applicants to be considered will have already been identified.

To work around these obstacles, you need to adopt a more narrowly tailored approach. This means (1) expending resources to identify the vacant positions for which you are most qualified, and (2) presenting your qualifications to the decision maker within the parameters we have discussed. How do you do that? The first step is to make a list of companies that are (1) the least likely to disqualify you from consideration due to your age and (2) the most likely to have vacancies that match your skills. The companies that fit these parameters are going to be the most likely to make you that job offer and are, therefore, the companies that you will want to target.

> "Insanity: doing the same thing over and over again and expecting different results."
> ALBERT EINSTEIN

OBJECTIVE INDICATORS OF MINIMAL AGEISM

If you have read this far, you should be less concerned about how your age will impact your job search because you know how to manage that part of the process. However, just as with any obstacle, if there are opportunities to avoid it, you should do so. Because of this, your target list should certainly include those companies that will be most likely to welcome your application. There are some subtle ways to assess whether an employer will be more or less likely to consider older candidates. For example, if you know a company has a reputation for hiring younger workers, either because its youthful culture is tightly engrained in its brand or because of anecdotal evidence that comes to your attention, then do not waste your time or resources trying to pursue an opportunity there. In addition, when you see advertisements seeking a recent college graduate, a maximum number of years of experience, or a maximum number of past employers, these stipulations all suggest that the employer is attempting to either intentionally or unintentionally discourage older candidates from applying. The term *digital native* seems to be a pretext for age discrimination, encouraging those who grew up immersed in technology and social media to respond to the posting.

Along these same lines, you may want to target employers that will see your age as an asset, such as organizations that handle age-related issues or tend to cater to the aging population. For example, the Equal Employment Opportunity Commission, which is the federal agency charged with enforcing the federal laws that prohibit age discrimination, is less likely to discriminate based on age than a cable station that targets viewers in the teenage demographic.

WHAT'S GOOD FOR THE GOOSE…

Another thing to keep in mind: While federal law makes it illegal for most employers to discriminate against individuals who are forty years of age and older, many state laws also prohibit employers from taking *anyone's* age into consideration. This means that just as employers are prohibited from eliminating older candidates based on their age, they are also prohibited from excluding younger candidates based on theirs. Consequently, even if an employer preferred to hire an older candidate, the decision is not always that simple. This legal reality prevents employers who have historically recognized (or, at least, because of the loyalty-free workplace, are continuing to recognize) the benefits of hiring an older candidate from making this objective known.

> Alex Dader owns one of the largest medical supply companies and sells chair lifts to the aging population. Looking to expand his sales team, Alex hopes to hire older candidates who not only have sales experience but who may have firsthand knowledge of the benefits of these lifts, as well as the other products sold by the company.

Despite this hiring need, Alex is unlikely to advertise for older candidates because he knows that this can cause him a legal headache. So, what does this means in practice? Put simply, employers who view you as the ideal candidate may be looking for you just as much as you are looking for them. Companies that work with products and services designed for older individuals, whether that be clothing, medical devices, or insurance products, might be incredibly receptive to older candidates because of the personal real-life experience you may have with their products as well as the problems their products are attempting to solve. However, this does not necessarily mean that they will be vocalizing this interest in older candidates because of the potential legal ramifications of doing so. Because of this, you will want to be sure to think about these types of companies when creating your target list, and you should especially target these companies if you are aware of a special skill that you have that can provide them with an immediate and valuable benefit.

TARGET COMPANIES THAT ARE MOST LIKELY TO HAVE A NEED FOR YOUR SKILLS

In addition to targeting companies that will be most receptive to older candidates, you will want to target companies that may have a need for your skills and level of experience.

> Jennifer Beederman, 52, has two decades of experience managing the human resources functions of a national company that started with two local offices but has grown to sixty-eight offices around the country, including some acquired from other companies and some she built from the ground up.

Given her vast experience, Jennifer has the potential to benefit the human resources department of any company. Her unique skills, however, indicate that she is capable of building the human resources functions of a new company, as well as merging existing policies and procedures with newly introduced policies. This makes her a particularly appealing candidate not only for companies that require the coordination of multiple offices, but any start-up company that is looking to build out its human resources department. Armed with that knowledge (along with some basic Internet research, and reading a few business publications), she can create a list of companies that fit these specifications and see if they have any vacancies that are a Cinderella fit for her qualifications.

THE DOWNSIDE OF THINKING BIG

If you are like most job hunters, you may be inclined to target larger employers first, based on the belief that the more individuals a company employs, the more vacancies it will likely have. This is sound thinking, except that most large companies tend to fill job openings by hiring or promoting from within their organization. And, the more employees the company has, the more likely the company will be able to find an internal candidate to fill any upcoming vacancies. Why? For one thing, the company already has firsthand knowledge of a current employee's job qualifications, work ethic, and ability to fit their corporate culture. This places external candidates at a significant disadvantage, especially if the company is very particular about how its employees complete their work, is looking for a very specific skill, or engages in a business that serves a particular niche. In addition, larger companies are more likely to have resources to train employees to qualify them for promotional opportunities, which will enable them to maintain a robust pipeline of qualified candidates to source for vacancies.

If an employer has a reputation for promoting from within, either with or without this expenditure of resources, this benefits current employees, so if you happen to be currently working for such an employer, by all means take advantage of that. However, if you are an older external candidate trying to penetrate an employer that adopts this mindset, you are at a significant disadvantage. This is because older candidates tend to be qualified for more senior positions and the more senior the position, the more likely the company will already have a pool of current employees in more junior roles who may be qualified for the position. If a junior position becomes available, the company will be more likely to recruit from the external applicant pool because there will be fewer internal candidates looking to move into those positions. (And, if you have senior-level experience, you do not necessarily want to target junior-level positions, as discussed in the previous chapter.)

THE UPSIDE OF THINKING SMALL

Given this mindset among big companies, in many cases it makes more sense for older candidates to target smaller employers. You will not only minimize the odds of facing such obstacles, but you will gain a number of strategic advantages. For one, because a smaller company is small, they may not have as large of a pipeline of qualified candidates to choose from. Therefore, they may be more receptive to hiring an outsider with your wealth of knowledge and experience for a senior role.

In addition, since smaller companies have smaller staffs and fewer resources to train new hires, they will be attracted to the idea that you will be able to walk in the door on day one with the skills necessary to complete the job.

Brandon Herbert, 55, is a professor with more than twenty years of experience teaching in a large academic institution in a large city. When Brandon and his wife decide to move to the country, where they hope to eventually retire, he applies to two large universities and three small liberal arts schools in the area. Brandon receives three job offers from the three liberal arts schools.

The larger institutions likely receive stacks of resumes for their vacancies, making those positions incredibly competitive. For this reason, it is possible that Brandon's application was never reviewed, or that some of the objective qualifications the institution used to narrow its applicant pool eliminated Brandon from consideration. However, it is likely that the smaller schools received far fewer applications than their larger counterparts, and fewer applications means less competition. Brandon's experience in a prestigious school likely made him an incredibly attractive candidate for a smaller school that might not regularly hear from people with that type of experience.

Consider this: If you are an interior designer, and you are talking to other interior designers about how to decorate a home on a shoestring budget, depending on your level of expertise, you may not stand out from the others. But, if you are in a room full of first-time homeowners and you relay that same information, they are going to be drawn to your experience because you know something they do not. The point is, if you have a lot of experience, a smaller company might be more willing to review your resume because they do not usually get inquiries from people with comparable qualifications.

In most cases, these smaller companies will be less well known, but a basic Google search will provide you with some information in no time at all. Most companies, even the smallest ones, have websites and some type of LinkedIn presence. Since LinkedIn will even help you search for companies based on the number of employees, you can easily target your search to those that will likely see the value of your decades of experience.

Once you identify your target company list, go to their websites, search for positions that match your qualifications, and apply. Use the cover letter and resume strategies discussed, and present yourself as a vibrant applicant who is the Cinderella fit for the available positions.

CONFIRM THAT YOUR RESUME TRACKS THE TRACKER

As you are preparing your online application, keep in mind that every company has people and processes whose sole purpose is to narrow the applicant pool down to a select number of candidates. In some cases, that gatekeeper is a computer program, known as an applicant tracking system (ATS). An ATS sorts through resumes and cover letters, looking for certain keywords, qualifications, years of experience, former employers, and whatever other criteria the prospective employer deems most relevant in determining possible matches for the position. Therefore, you need to make sure that your resume and application registers a high enough score with the ATS to ensure your application gets through this initial level of review.

How do you do that? By thinking like a computer database. Since most databases are only as good as the information contained within them, you want to tailor your resume so that it mimics the information that is included in the job posting. This means using the exact words in the job description in your resume and avoiding any abbreviations or acronyms. In addition, because the ATS will be scanning your resume for relevance, you want to pepper your resume with certain keywords (which you can easily find by searching job postings for similar positions). So if you are applying for a senior editor position with a lifestyle and entertainment magazine your application should include "lifestyle," "entertainment," "Associated Press," "Associated Press Stylebook," and "senior editor," as well as keywords such as "celebrities," "movies," "nightlife," "music," "health," and other departments that you would typically find in a similar publication. If it is a sophisticated ATS, it may also look for industry-specific qualifications such as the achievement of certain certifications, recognizable trainings, and affiliations with certain associations. If any of these items apply to your background, include them in your application.

Along the same lines, since most tracking systems are programmed to track certain information, be sure to use conventional headings in your resume (such as "career objective," "professional experience" and "education") that the system is likely to recognize. This also means avoiding pictures, images, and graphics—all of which will appear like gobbledygook once they are run through the system—as well as headers and footers.

All of your essential information, such as your phone number and e-mail address, should appear in the body of the resume. Finally, left justify the resume text (which is usually the default setting in most programs), and use a standard font such as Times New Roman.

Remember, you want your resume to be seen by an individual, which will not happen unless it gets past the computer system first. Even if you pride yourself on being unconventional, you need to follow certain conventions if you want to make the cut. (And, of course you will also want to utilize the other cover letter and resume strategies discussed in Strategy #1 and its postscript in order to increase the likelihood you will receive this result).

USE YOUR NETWORK TO GET NOTICED

Of course, you do not just want your resume to be seen by *any* individual. You want it seen by *the right* individual. This is particularly important for older candidates, because face time with the hiring manager or head of human resources can make all the difference in whether your application is given its appropriate consideration. But, because of the sheer number of job applications for any given position, even if your application gets past the online system, there is still no guarantee it will be reviewed.

> Dave Bester is recruiting for a front desk agent for a large hotel chain. The job is posted on a Monday. By Friday afternoon, the ATS has identified thirty-six potentially qualified candidates for the position. Dave tells the recruiters to send him those thirty-six resumes and to hold all other applications until he requests them. Dave reviews the thirty-six resumes and selects three to move forward in the process.

The reality is that the applicant pool may consist of a number of qualified candidates. Once a recruiter starts to review the ATS-approved resumes, that person may stop reviewing resumes once a certain number of potentially qualified candidates are identified. He can always return to the applicant pool if someone from that initial applicant pool is not offered

**"I did some networking with someone I knew
as a kid. My imaginary friend got me a job
as an imaginary account executive."**

the position. For this reason, it is critical that you not only reach out to your network when you identify a vacant position, but that you reach out to them as early as possible and in a way that is most likely to generate an efficient response. Few things are as irritating as setting a time to speak with a potential candidate, only to realize that they did not provide a phone number where they can be reached at the scheduled time, or that the person forgot about the appointment. Approach a discussion with someone in your network with the same level of professionalism that you would when reporting to an interview. This way, your connections will be comfortable providing you with the best possible advice and suggestions as to how you can move to the next step.

In addition, when asking someone for a favor, make it as easy as possible for the person to help you as quickly as possible. Otherwise, you may lose out on the value of your connection because you did not act quickly enough.

> Kat Watchman, 60, applies for a position as the director of communications for a large transportation company after finding the position advertised on the company's website. Kat applies for the position and reaches out to James Ables, a childhood friend who, she learns through LinkedIn, currently works for the company in a satellite

office. Ten days after Kat sends her e-mail, James apologizes for the delayed response as he does not regularly check his LinkedIn account and tells Kat that he is friendly with the human resources recruiter and would be willing to forward her application to him. Three days later, Kat provides this information to John; ten days later, when John checks his e-mail, he forwards her application. John receives a response from the recruiter that, although he has already selected his slate of candidates who will be interviewed, he will consider Kat if the company does not find an appropriate candidate from those interviews.

In this case, Kat was faced with a few obstacles, most of which could have been avoided. Since she was basically asking John to forward her application to the hiring manager, her initial e-mail to him should have included the position title, her online confirmation number, and a copy of the cover letter and resume she submitted. Not only that, she should have drafted the e-mail in a professional manner so that the moment John received her e-mail and realized it was something he was willing to do, he could have forwarded her application along. In addition, since Kat knew James rarely checked his LinkedIn e-mail account after his first reply, she should have tried to find an alternative e-mail address (or, at least, called him directly to find out the most efficient way to provide the follow-up information).

Having to connect with a person twice only doubles the chances that he either does not have the time to complete the request or may have intentionally or unintentionally ignored it. In this case, the delay prevented Kat from being considered with the initial batch of candidates.

HOW TO REACH THE DECISION MAKER

Granted, all is not lost for Kat, since she may still be called in for an interview. Even so, she spent a lot of time and effort without any guarantee that the hiring manager will even know that she applied for the director of communications position. Is there any way she could have bypassed the ATS system and human resources and reached out to the hiring manager directly? The answer to that is yes.

Erika Winters, 58, applies for a position as an accounts payable clerk. Since Erika knows that most companies require applicants to apply for vacant positions through their website, she submits a cover letter and resume through the online system. Besides applying online, Erika reaches out to a former colleague who works at the company to tell her she applied for the position and would welcome an introduction to the hiring manager. Through this connection, Erika interviews with the hiring manager and is invited back for a second interview. The day Erika is scheduled to return to the company for the second interview, she receives a generic e-mail from the company's online application system indicating that, despite her qualifications, the company has determined there are other candidates who are more suitable. Erika ignores the notification, participates in the second round of interviews, and is offered the position.

This goes back to the point we made earlier about job listings that are posted on traditional forums: In many cases, by the time these openings are posted, the position may have already been filled as a result of a parallel process such as the one that allowed Erika to reach out to the hiring manager directly.

While this may seem unfair, remember that searching for a job is no different than any other competition: You need to understand the rules and strategies in order to succeed. If you are an older candidate, reaching out to the hiring manager directly can be particularly beneficial for the following reasons:

1. *By contacting a hiring manager directly, you are showing the decision maker that you are truly interested in the position, because you made the effort to connect with the correct people.* These are precisely the traits employers look for in their prospective employees.

2. *By reaching out to a hiring manager directly, you show yourself to be a go-getter—someone with the drive, energy, and determination to get the job done.* Not only will this disavow any preconceived notions the hiring manager may have related to your age, it will increase your chances of getting in front of the actual decision maker, which is what you ultimately want.

3. *A hiring manager may be just as eager to truncate the system as you.* Remember, hiring managers are inundated with resumes for any given position. Having sat on that side of the desk myself, I can tell you that many people would love nothing more than to find the best candidate possible without having to review stacks of resumes from unqualified applicants.

> Mia Dotson is hiring a new account executive for her national furniture store. Mia posts the job vacancy online on Friday afternoon. When she returns to work on Monday morning, she finds that 118 applicants applied for the position. By Thursday, the number has climbed to 201 applications. By the time she starts to review the applicant pool on Friday morning, she had received three e-mail messages and two voicemail messages from former colleagues alerting her to the fact that someone they know has applied for the position. Mia pulls those five applications from the file, determines that three are potentially qualified, and invites them for an interview. Mia hires a candidate from that group of three.

This also speaks to a complaint that I often hear from clients: "I sent the company my application, but I never received a response." In response, I usually tell them, "Do not take it personally," because chances are their applications were never even reviewed, for reasons we just discussed. That being the case, it becomes even more critical for older candidates to reach out to hiring managers directly.

As another example, imagine that you run a large manufacturing department and need a labor attorney to help you negotiate the various collective bargaining agreements with each labor union. Following your company's protocol, you reach out to human resources to set up interviews. Some candidates are employment attorneys with extensive experience in workplace issues. Others are attorneys with extensive experience in negotiating contracts. None of the candidates presented to you, however, have the specific skill set you need.

Granted, it is entirely possible that, for whatever reason, there just are not any qualified candidates actively looking for new opportunities at that time. It is also possible, however, that your HR recruiter may not understand that negotiating union contracts is a specialized skill, and as a result, may be eliminating candidates who are actually an ideal fit without even realizing it.

Now, what if your cousin Lucy happens to tell you that her husband who has twenty-five years of experience negotiating collective bargaining agreements with unions is currently looking for a job? Given the circumstances, you would probably jump at the opportunity to hear from him directly and possibly grant him an interview. In this case, while Lucy's husband may feel uneasy about approaching the hiring manager directly, it may be the exact result the hiring manager is hoping for.

HOW TO CONNECT WITH THE DECISION MAKER: OVER, UNDER, THROUGH

Of course, it is one thing to understand the value of connecting with the hiring manager, and it is another thing to be able to find out their identity. The good news, however, is that there are a number of strategies you can use to uncover this incredibly valuable piece of information.

You may not find that person's name in the job posting, but more often than not it will include clues to their identity. For example, a posting for a transportation coordinator might include such language as "reporting to the Executive Vice-President of Transportation, the person hired into this role will...." Voila! You have the title of the decision maker. Now all you need is their name and their contact information. In some cases, this is as easy as picking up the phone, calling the main number of the company, and asking for the name of the Executive Vice-President of Transportation. Most receptionists will comply. If the phone is answered by someone who declines to provide this information, call again after business hours—some companies permit you to search their directory by job title, allowing you to reach the voicemail of that person (which, presumably, will begin with their name).

> "Obstacles do not have to stop you. If you run into a wall, don't turn around and give up. Figure out how to climb it, go through it, or work around it."
> MICHAEL JORDAN

In some cases, the job posting may not include a name or title, but it will list a fax number. Do a Google search on that number and see if a name comes up. If the posting includes a job title, but not the name of the company, there are still ways to identify the right person. Suppose the ad begins with "SPF is a media company seeking an account executive" in whatever town or city you live in. Do an online search of the yellow pages to see if you can figure out the name, and if that does not work, pull out a phonebook (or go to your nearest public library and ask to use their phonebook) and see if you can find a company with the initials SPF under the media section, then follow the steps outlined above.

If you cannot find the name of the hiring manager by contacting the company directly, go to the company's website or LinkedIn page. Many companies post management bios on their website, so if the person has a high-level position you should be able to find them there. If the hiring manager does not hold a senior position, no worries—if the company website includes a staff directory or an organizational chart, that should provide you with the name (and possibly contact information) of the person you want.

If you are targeting a hiring manager at a large company, you should be able to find that person through Hoovers, a paid service that provides proprietary business information on more than 85 million corporations. (If you do not subscribe to Hoovers, see if your library does.) If that does not work, purchase the latest copy of a trade publication. Most such magazines include columns that are dedicated to identifying the hirings, resignations, and promotions of people within and among different companies. Not only that, but reading trade publications will keep you on top of the latest industry trends. This knowledge will come in handy once you connect with the hiring manager and in your future interviews.

If all else fails, some simple Internet research might do the trick. Search for industry-specific organizational charts with common reporting structures, then try to pinpoint a name from there. Even if you are not completely certain that the person you identify is the person you want, by connecting with someone in a similar role at the company you have at least increased the chances that your application and materials will get into the right hands.

Once you have hit the bullseye, your next step is to make a personal connection with the hiring manager. Look them up on LinkedIn and see if you have any connections in common. If you do, ask one of your connections to arrange for an introduction. This will be the most direct way to gain access to hiring managers. (In some cases, companies offer referral fees to employees who recommend a candidate who is eventually hired. So if you cannot connect with the manager directly, one of his employees might assist you, if only because there is a financial incentive.) The key here is knowing the difference between persistence and being a pest. If none of these steps work, cross this name off your list and try to connect with the hiring manager at another company.

IF THE DOOR IS OPEN, WALK IN

Now suppose you visit the hiring manager's LinkedIn profile and see them identified as an "open networker." This is good news for you, because it means that that they are open to connecting with anyone who is interested in connecting with them. That being the case, personalize your invitation to connect. The key word here is *personalize*—do not just sending a generic "I would like to connect" invitation. By taking a few extra minutes to indicate your interest in the specific vacancy and asking whether they might be willing to speak with you for a few minutes about it, you are showing the hiring manager that you were willing to go the extra mile to make the connection. That also tells them what sort of employee you would be, as we have discussed before.

If the hiring manager is not an open networker, see if their profile includes an option to "follow" them. That option allows you to read their update posts, rather than being a direct connection. (As you can imagine, this is similar to following the person on Twitter, which you should also do if you find that they have an account there.)

While you are at it, Google the person to see what else you might learn about them. For example, if the hiring manager is scheduled to speak at a conference next month in your city, mention that in your cover letter requesting an in-person meeting or telephone call—which might lend itself to other points of access. Or, better yet, try to attend the conference yourself. Conferences are a great way to connect with people with whom you might not otherwise connect. At the very least, it will allow you to introduce yourself to the hiring manager, as well as meet other people who might make valuable additions to your network.

If you cannot connect with the hiring manager on LinkedIn (or cannot find their e-mail address on the company website, and do not know any-one who happens to work at that same company), you can likely find it by running a Google search with "@" and the company's domain name. This will give you the company's e-mail address format, which can lead you to the hiring manager. So if the company's website is *www.amazing-jobfinder.com*, a Google search for *@amazingjobfinder.com* should produce at least one address, such as *Sarah.Jones@amazingjobfinder.com*. This tells you that the company's e-mail format is the employee's first name and last name, separated by a period. (If you want to make sure that such an e-mail address exists, go to *http://verify-email.org*, a free service.)

Once you identify the hiring manager, if you really want to set yourself apart, consider sending your cover letter and resume via snail mail in addition to following the directions included in the job posting. At the very least, your communications will stand out from among the dozens (and, likely, hundreds) of e-mail applications the hiring manager receives. Personalize the letter to the extent you can, using the ideas we have just discussed, and make sure it looks professional without any spelling or grammatical errors.

Now, some of you may ask, "What about dropping by the office myself and delivering my materials in person?" While that will certainly get the decision maker's attention, I usually do not recommend this strat-egy because it can just as easily backfire and reflect poorly on you. For one, people are busy. You cannot assume that they will be available to meet with you when you drop by their office unannounced. Now, if you are targeting a specific company that happens to encourage such aggressive strategies, by all means go for it. As a general rule, though, you are more likely to yield the results you want by adopting a more professional approach.

NOTHING VENTURED, NOTHING GAINED

Granted, by circumventing protocol and reaching out to the hiring manager directly, you are taking a calculated risk—especially if the job posting specifically states that applicants should not call about the position or contact the company directly. In my opinion, however, if you are a candidate of a certain age, it is worth the risk because the alternative is to rely on the traditional process (which, especially for older candidates, presents unique challenges). More to the point, reaching out directly to the person hiring for a specific job is a great way to show that decision maker why you are the perfect fit for the position and that nothing about your age should disqualify you. In the race against all other applicants vying for the same position, such a move can give you the inside track and make all the difference.

So far, this discussion presumes that you find some vacancies at some of the companies that you target. Depending on your line of work and the size of the companies you target, I would venture to say that most companies have at least some vacancies at any given time. They just may not need to advertise them broadly because they receive so many applications from their website traffic. Therefore, unless you go to their website, you will never learn about those opportunities. But, of course, some of you may say, "What if I go to their websites and they have no vacancies?" Granted, there is always this possibility. Even so, the work you did to create this target list still has the potential to produce some results.

DO NOT GIVE UP PREMATURELY

Suppose that you do not find any appropriate vacancies at the ten companies on your list or, the more likely result, which is that you find a few vacancies at some of the companies but no vacancies at the others. What do you do with the rest of your targets? Toss them aside? Not necessarily. Find a way to "stay in touch" with the online job postings so that you will be notified when the positions for which you are the most qualified become vacant. One way to do this is to create a master online profile, which most company websites will let you do, even if there are no current openings that match your qualifications. This way, when an appropriate position does become available, the company will notify you and you can return to the website to submit your formal application.

Creating a master online profile will provide other valuable information that you can use in your job search. For one, when completing your profile, the website will ask how you heard about the employer or the particular job opening. More often

> "I will prepare and someday my chance will come."
> ABRAHAM LINCOLN

than not, you will see a drop-down menu with options (e.g., did you hear about us through LinkedIn, or a job search website like Indeed.com, or by attending a specific conference or job fair). Once you come across that list, take a screen shot of that drop-menu and focus your attention on every single option on the list. Chances are, these are places where the employer is most likely to recruit for its vacant positions. If one such conference or job fair happens to take place in your city, it might be worth your while to attend it and make some connections.

Finally, do not leave anything to chance. Even if you set up your master application to inform you of appropriate positions in the future, drop by the website on a regular basis to see whether anything has changed. For all its efficiency, the automated notification system may somehow overlook an opportunity that may be perfect for you. Not only that, but by visiting the website yourself, you will learn about the types of vacancies that are most common. If you go back to the website over an extended period of time and see the same jobs over and over (but the system did not tell you about them because you do not appear to be qualified for them), see if there is a way in which you *can* become qualified and apply for them.

So far, we have focused on how to approach and compete for positions that have been posted or that you expect to be posted in the future. There are, however, a host of other employment opportunities that are vacant now that most job seekers do not know about because they can only be found in the hidden job market. How to access the hidden job market, which will enable you to avoid the line of qualified candidates as opposed to strategizing to be at the front of it, is mapped out next in Strategy #5.

STRATEGY #5

EXCAVATE THE
BURIED TREASURES

"If your ship doesn't come in, swim out to it."
—Jonathan Winters

The hidden job market is a wealth of opportunities that are not yet advertised, as well as jobs that applicants proactively create where none currently exist. This process virtually eliminates a number of obstacles that you would ordinarily face and have to expend precious resources to overcome. In the hidden market, there are no gatekeepers to bypass because you will have eliminated the gates. The way you break down these barriers to entry is by placing your resume directly into the hands of the decision makers that you have determined will be most likely to make you a job offer.

One significant benefit of the hidden job market is that not only will applicants get to the hiring manager well in advance of the competition, in many situations there will be no competition at all: You are in control of the process. In most cases, you will be approaching the hiring manager before he has a vacancy to fill or realizes how he can benefit from the creation of a new role that just happens to be a perfect fit for your qualifications. And because you will only be targeting the opportunities for which you are the Cinderella fit, this will greatly increase your chances of receiving an offer.

Knowing about the hidden job market and how to tap into it is a good thing—especially if you are an older candidate. Instead of pitching yourself for a position where your age may be seen as a

> "If you genuinely want something, don't wait for it—teach yourself to be impatient."
> GURBAKSH CHAHAL

detriment, you are essentially making a pitch for a position for which only you qualify. Despite these significant advantages, you would be surprised at how many job seekers resist the idea. Some say that it is hard enough finding a job among the vacancies that do exist—they do not have time to go on a scavenger hunt for opportunities that may never materialize. Others believe that if employers have hidden certain jobs from the public, they hid them for a reason and may not want outsiders to find them. Regardless of whether these are wise or accurate characterizations of the process, they are beside the point.

Remember, the modern workplace is loyalty-free. Like it or not, some hiring managers will intentionally or even unintentionally consider your age when determining whether to hire you. And, employers want what employers want. They may not have the time, energy, or inclination to take a more creative approach to the hiring process. You can complain about the unfairness of the system (and continue to have difficulties finding your next job), or you can look for ways to make the system work for you. Speaking from experience, I have found it is better to focus on the latter, because it will exponentially increase your chances of finding your next job and earning your perpetual paycheck.

Besides, hiring managers work in the same loyalty-free workplace that you do. Meaning, it takes time for them to find the perfect fit for any given vacancy—and the time they spend sifting through resumes, setting up interviews, and meeting with candidates is time away from the other responsibilities they have to meet in order to do their job (and keep *their* bosses happy). By inserting yourself into the process—which is basically what you are doing when you reach out to hiring managers before vacancies are announced—you are actually doing the hiring managers a favor, while also starting the process from a position of strength.

WHY THESE JOBS ARE HIDDEN

That said, you cannot make the system work for you unless you understand how the system works. So let's take a look at some of the reasons why employers hide certain jobs in the first place.

One fall I was speaking with the sales director of a gym about the best time of year to sign up for a new membership. Like most people, I figured

I would wait until January to take advantage of any upcoming sales. "You could do that," said the director, "but it likely will not get you the best deal." He went on to tell me that because people often think about getting into shape after the holidays, most gyms will not offer specials as the new year approaches because they do not need to: They almost always see a spike in new memberships at that time. "If you are really looking for a bargain," the director went on to say, "sign up in the middle of summer. Because people are exercising outdoors and enjoying the weather, gym attendance is usually low. That is when you will find your best deals."

How is this relevant to your job search process? Just as a gym has no need to spend money on advertising in January, companies that are well known, and/or have a reputation for being stellar employers, do not need to advertise their positions because everyone wants to work for them anyway. When they do have a vacancy, instead of posting an ad on a popular job board, which will open the floodgates to both qualified and unqualified job applicants, they simply recruit candidates from the overflowing pool of resumes that they already have on file. This means the job will be filled before you are aware it is vacant, which further illustrates the importance of tapping into this hidden market.

Now, in some situations, a job may be hidden even though the employer did not intend for that to be the result.

Suppose your friend Tracy owns a mid-sized home health aide company and is looking to hire two new aides, as well as a new office manager. She posts the opportunities on her website, but receives no responses. On the one hand, it is entirely possible that no one wants to work for her company. The more likely reason for the absence of applicants is that Tracy's website does not generate a lot of traffic (and, therefore, few job hunters would think of going there to look for job openings). Technically speaking, that makes all three positions hidden opportunities.

The good news: If you are a candidate of a certain age, and are interested in any of these vacancies, you may have little, if any, competition. This is why older candidates should be targeting these types of smaller companies. The bad news: You still have to find them in order to apply.

In other cases, if a company is looking to hire someone with a specific skill set—such as a private consultant who specializes in helping operations run more efficiently—they may not want to make that open-ing public because of what it might do to the workforce. Think about it: If employees knew about potential changes that might impact their employment, they might start looking for opportunities with other employers. That, in turn, affects production, which in turn will affect the company's bottom line.

Then again, if you are in the market for a new job (and somehow learned that the company is looking to hire someone with just your type of back-ground), it might be worth reaching out to the company proactively and discretely to illustrate the immediate value you can bring.

A related situation may materialize on a much smaller scale:

> Lynda Khan, 38, the national sales director for a cosmetic line, has not been meeting her sales targets for an extended period of time. The company has spoken with Lynda about her performance, but as she has not shown any signs of improvements, they are looking to replace her.

In this situation, the company may conclude that, despite Lynda's inadequate performance, it is in their best interest to keep her in the senior position until they identify and hire her replacement. Therefore, the company would probably conduct a hidden (and almost invisible) search. Even if Lynda knows that her future with the company is not certain, the last thing the company would want is for her to realize just how dire her situation is by seeing her own job posted on the most popular job boards.

In others cases, a company may conduct a hidden search by mutual consent:

> Paul O'Neil, 66, is the CEO of an online learning plat-form, which he built into a multimillion-dollar business during the time he served in that role. Though Paul has indicated his intent to retire from the position, he and the company agree that his departure will not be announced until a successor is identified.

In this situation, Paul may be very loyal to the company he built and therefore wants to ensure its continued success after his departure. For these reasons, he may want the search for his successor to be hidden to prevent panic from not only from current employees, but also from customers, advertisers, and shareholders who might be concerned about a lack of leadership for even a short period of time.

Each of these situations represents a job vacancy that could be the perfect opportunity for one of the countless frustrated job applicants who has continued to mass e-mail their resumes to recruiters in the hopes of landing an interview. And, if you are a candidate who limits their job search to the vacancies you can find on job boards, you will be joining in on their frustration and missing each and every one of these pristine opportunities.

Another source of valuable opportunities you will miss out on if you do not target the hidden job market are those that an employer might be willing to create just for you.

WHEN SOMEONE KNOCKS ON YOUR DOOR, ANSWER IT

Another advantage of implementing the strategies designed to target the hidden job market is that sometimes an employer meets a candidate who can add immediate value, so he creates a position for her, even if there is not a vacancy.

> Marisol Moller, the academic chair of an online business school, has four full-time faculty members, each of whom has broad expertise in the unique learning platform implemented by the school. Each semester, Marisol struggles to appropriately staff her classes, but she simply does not have the time to recruit and train another staff member to use the delivery system. Upon receiving a cover letter and resume from an individual with more than twenty years of experience working on the exact delivery system used by the college, Marisol invites the candidate in for an interview and extends him an offer.

Timing is everything. While Marisol was not actively looking to expand her staff (and, therefore, did not formally post a vacancy on the school's website), when she happened to find a qualified candidate who could hit the ground running, she was more than happy to create a position for him.

As we mentioned before, finding the Cinderella fit is often a long, drawn-out process from the company's perspective. Just thinking about having to recruit for a position is enough to compel a hiring manager to continue with its existing staff. In fact, in many cases, just as we saw with Marisol, when a hiring manager identifies qualified candidates, she is more than happy to create positions for them now, rather than having to engage in the process later.

> Jill Austin has a vacancy in her customer service depart-
> ment that has taken close to eighteen months to fill,
> largely because the position requires the candidate to
> work a number of overnight shifts to properly supervise
> the 24-hour operation. When Jill receives an inquiry from
> an individual who expresses an interest in an overnight
> position (because she shares the childcare responsibilities
> with her husband who works during the day), Jill invites
> the candidate in for an interview.

Here again, an interview is extended even though there is no current vacancy because Jill wants a candidate in the pipeline in the event an overnight position is vacated. If someone does resign, that job will likely never even be posted because Jill can immediately reach out to the individual who previously expressed interest in the job. If that candidate is available, Jill can fill the position immediately, without having to embark on another exhaustive search. This will enable her to avoid the stress of having the job unfilled for the time it takes her to conduct a search, or having to fill the job with a mediocre candidate who represents the best available option from the current applicant pool.

The point is that just because you do not see a vacancy listed on a company website, this does not mean that one does not exist. If you have a skill set or something about you that makes you the ideal candidate to work for a particular company, you need to be proactive about reaching out to them to see if there might be a hidden opportunity that is a fit.

NOT ALL HIDDEN OPPORTUNITIES ARE OUTSIDE YOUR VIEW

In some situations, the best jobs in the hidden job market are not hidden at all. This is because the greatest source of hidden job opportunities is usually at the company where you currently work. If you are unhappy with your current position, there may be other opportunities with your current employer in a different department, or a different role, or a different office. If you are not earning a competitive salary (or your level of compensation has peaked), you might be able to earn more by transferring to another area of the company. If you like your job, but do not get along with your boss, a transfer to a new department could resolve the situation.

This is not to say that you should stop looking for opportunities at another company if you think that is your best option. If you go that route, just know that you will have to overcome many of the obstacles regarding your age that we have discussed in this book—whereas if you pursue another position with your current employer, those obstacles will likely not even exist. Why? Because you are a known entity with a proven track record of performance. The company will not have to worry about whether you fit into its culture, while you know what it takes to work there and succeed.

As soon as you learn that someone at your company is being promoted, see if the position that person is vacating might represent a promotional opportunity for you. As a current employee, you should have a sense of where the best opportunities are, and you should be able to pursue them before any outsiders even know they are available. Aside from the fact that you have access to information to which outsiders are not privy, you also know what it takes to get hired by that company because they have already hired you!

Even if there are not any vacancies that you know of, it might be time for you to discuss a promotion. In many cases, a salary increase and title change are enough to satisfy even the most ambitious job-seekers.

If you receive performance-based bonuses, workplace perks, and positive feedback throughout the year, you might consider asking about any promotional opportunities during your next performance evaluation. If, despite your good performance, you continue to be passed over for promotions (or were never considered for them in the first place), consider whether you are involved in meetings or even invited to participate. If the answer is yes, there may still be room for growth. If the answer is no, perhaps the best hidden opportunity will be one with a different employer.

SMALL TALK CAN LEAD TO BIG OPPORTUNITIES

I once attended a panel discussion for aspiring scriptwriters. Near the end of the discussion, one of the attendees asked the moderator, an established scriptwriter, how to 100 percent guarantee that no one in Hollywood would steal his script, which he was certain would eventually become the next blockbuster. The moderator asked if the script had been written and printed out. The answer to both was yes.

"Perfect," said the moderator. "When you get home, erase any digital copies, place the printed copy carefully under your bedroom mattress, and keep it there forever. This is your 100 percent guarantee the idea will not be stolen by anyone in Hollywood. Unfortunately, this is also the only 100 percent guarantee that your script will never be made into a movie."

OK, perhaps the moderator was being overly dramatic, but you get the point. If you want someone to buy your script, you have to let them know it is available.

How does this translate to the hidden job market? Well, that is pretty simple: The best way to learn about any possible vacancies is to let others know you are looking for one.

People who are already employed often hesitate to let others know they are looking for a job, for fear that their boss might find out. Or, if they have been laid off or terminated, they are too embarrassed or depressed to talk about it with others. Unfortunately, unless you open up to others at some point, the odds of finding the job you want are about as good as Steven Spielberg discovering your screenplay that you have hidden it under your mattress. Unless you reach out to people, whether you are employed or not, you will not be in a position to receive any leads if and when they materialize. The more you talk about the fact that you are looking for a position, the more opportunities you will learn about. Remember, hidden jobs will not come to you, you have to go to them.

One great source of hidden job opportunities is small talk. Yes, in many situations it really is that simple.

> At Thanksgiving dinner, business executive Terrence Samuels, 71, toasts to his plan to be fully retired by their next Turkey Day gathering. Harold Raven, 54, the husband of Terrence's cousin who is at the dinner, has a conversation with Terrence about his position. They agree to set up a meeting for the following week to discuss the potential opportunity.

In this case, had Harold not been assertive enough to approach Terrence after hearing his announcement, Harold might have never learned about the opportunity (had it not been advertised), or he might have submitted his application well after other qualified applicants had been identified.

This Thanksgiving dinner example shows not only the advantages of accessing the hidden job market, but the disadvantages of not tapping into it.

> "Success doesn't come to you. You go to it."
> MARVA COLLINS

It is natural for people to talk about their current jobs and future plans in ordinary conversations. These conversations can alert you to many job opportunities well in advance of when the active search begins, if there is a search at all. So, if you are privy to such an exchange, be like Harold and initiate the process to target a job (or in this case an upcoming vacancy) just as soon as opportunity presents itself. This will catapult you into the best position to be considered for the job.

Of course, you do not have to wait for pronouncements at the next holiday gathering. You can also learn about potentially hidden opportunities by reaching out to your network. In many cases, that can be as simple as keeping your ears open the next time you talk to your mailman, hair stylist, or the person sitting next to you on the train as you commute to work. When immersed in your job search, you never know where the next opportunity will come from. Each and every conversation you have may lead to information about a vacancy that is right for you.

> Jayne Baller, 37, an attorney for a large nonprofit organi-
> zation, wants her company to approve an increased head
> count so that she can hire another attorney to join her
> team. When the company finally approves her request,
> Jayne sends out an e-mail blast to her law school friends,
> saying that she's looking for a "superstar" attorney: "If you
> know anyone please send them my way, ASAP."

Jayne may not have intended this, but this is essentially a hidden job:
Unless you happen to have graduated from law school with Jayne, or are
somehow connected to someone who graduated with Jayne (and who
immediately thinks of you once they hear the job description), you are
not likely to know about it. Letting others know that you are looking for
a job and continuing to expand your network will increase the chances
that you will learn about these hidden opportunities.

If you are a candidate of a certain age, do not just talk to your contempo-
raries: Reach out to those who are younger than you. Talking to younger
people in your network not only provides you with access to new information, but can help shatter some of the perceptions about your age that
we have already discussed. If you are in your early fifties, and have a twen-
ty-seven-year-old niece who works in the same industry you do, reaching
out to her will let her know that you are open to the idea of working for
a younger boss. Should your niece hear of an opportunity in her network,
she will remember that and will not hesitate to alert you to the vacancy.

When sourcing opportunities from your network, be forthright. Ask them
if they know of any vacancies and be as specific as possible. (Remember,
hiring managers are looking for the Cinderella fit for their positions.
They are *not* looking for candidates who are so desperate that they will
do anything for anyone.) And, in the spirit of this chapter, do not just ask
about opportunities that have already been posted. The people in your
network might have information as to how you can access hidden opportunities at the companies where they have previously worked.

> Payroll specialist Brian Olsen, 55, is eager to find a posi-
> tion at a large manufacturing company that is located
> in the city where he is planning to relocate. Through a

LinkedIn search, he learns that a former colleague, Megan O'Leary, 54, worked for the company a number of years before. Though Megan informs Brian that she no longer has any contacts at the company, she adds that when she worked there, most of the new hires were people who the company met at the annual International Manufacturing Technology Show held each spring.

This goes back to the example in the previous chapter about the value of attending conferences. In this case, Brian learns that the real opportunities at this particular company stem from the annual trade show. If he is really committed to working for the company, he will find a way to go to the next year's show. If he is not, he can redirect his time and effort from finding vacancies on the website to other tasks that will more likely lead to viable opportunities.

STAY ON TOP OF THE NEWS

Besides targeting companies that appear to have no vacancies, pay attention to news trends in the industry in which you work. Set up a Google alert by entering keywords into a search string, then directing Google to e-mail you anytime there are articles that include those words. Then spend a few minutes each morning reviewing the breaking news on major websites that report on the industry where you plan to work. You may find indicators of current or future vacancies and be able to target them when they are still hidden, or at least not in full view.

IT specialist Sarah Nordic, 61, reads a newspaper article reporting on workplace perks of employers. According to the item, one technology company, Big Bytes, is seriously considering adopting a number of new family-friendly employment policies, such as paid family leave and onsite daycare, in order to compete with its competitors Technology Titans and Everything Electronics, both of which offer these types of benefits. Upon reading this article, Sarah immediately reaches out to her connections at Big Bytes to inquire about any job opportunities.

"Opportunity texted me, tweeted me, linked to me, friended me, blogged me and spammed me. I was expecting it to knock!"

After the publication of this article, Sarah knew that both Technology Titans and Everything Electronics will likely receive a surge of applicants for open positions based on their rich benefits offerings. Thus it makes sense for her to reach out to Big Bytes, the company that does not currently offer these perks. First, if most people reading the article apply for positions with the competitors, that automatically eliminates some of the competition for Big Bytes. More significant is what Sarah learns from reading between the lines of this article. If Big Bytes is considering adding such rich benefits, there is a strong possibility that the company is experiencing a high level of employee turnover and is looking for ways to maintain its staff. That tells Sarah that there may be vacancies at Big Bytes that are worth exploring.

When looking for hidden opportunities in the news about a particular company, also look for items that report significant growth and expansion in the company, as well as its entry into new business areas or acquisition of new products. Companies that report success in finding new investors or new funding sources will likely have hiring needs.

SOME HIDDEN OPPORTUNITIES
ARE RIGHT IN FRONT OF YOU

Another way to find new opportunities is to consider less traditional positions and working arrangements that you may not have previously considered. Many candidates of a certain age have only worked in traditional full-time positions with benefits. In the modern workplace, however, there are a host of great opportunities that do not fit within these parameters. A part-time position, for example, will not only enable you to earn some money during a transition, but provide an opportunity to develop new skills, which can bolster your resume. (This is particularly beneficial if you have received consistent feedback related to the absence of a certain skill.) In addition, from the point of view of a hiring manager looking to fill a full-time position, a candidate that is currently employed, even if in a part-time or temporary role, is usually considered a stronger candidate (and, therefore, more likely to receive an offer) than one who is unemployed. And, if you are working in a company in any capacity, you will be in a better position to find hidden job opportunities—even if a position is only hidden for a short period of time, starting from when an individual resigns and ending when the job posting is released and widely publicized. Finally, while few part-time jobs include benefits, once you prove your ability to do the work, it is possible that the position will be converted to a full-time position if your workload increases and additional funding becomes available.

> "Sometimes the questions are complicated and the answers are simple."
> DR. SEUSS

The same holds true for freelance positions and consulting projects. Both offer an income stream, the opportunity to develop new skills, and the potential to expand your network, which will increase your chances of learning about new opportunities. Not only that, but in many cases older candidates actually have an advantage in these hidden and less traditional roles because they have more flexibility in their schedules. Even if your goal is to secure a full-time position with benefits, these less traditional positions may get you one step closer to your ultimate goal.

As we previously discussed, you will want to target companies that cater to people in your demographic as part of their customer base. While in your prior research you may have created a targeted list of the more well-known companies that cater to an older customer base, remain alert to other lesser-known companies that may fit within these parameters.

> Content writer Sandra Nestler, 62, receives a sales call from a start-up company selling a new type of supplemental insurance designed for senior citizens who are unable to cover their full medical costs with government-sponsored programs. While Sandra is not interested in purchasing additional insurance, after receiving the sales pitch she sends a cover letter and resume to the head of the sales team (after finding his contact information on the company's website), suggesting that she could add significant value to the company because she has decades of experience creating customized content, and happens to be in the precise demographic the company is trying to target.

As an older candidate, you have the skills and experience to add value to an employer. By targeting employers whose products and services cater specifically to your demographic, you offer them not only the value of your experience, but the knowledge, familiarity, and understanding of their products and services and the role they play in your life—an added benefit that most employers will recognize.

MERGERS AND SPIN-OFFS

Another potential source of hidden opportunities is with companies that are undergoing significant changes, such as mergers or spin-offs. While that may seem counterintuitive at first (since most mergers result in the reduction of jobs), in some cases new partnerships may result in new opportunities for someone with your area of expertise.

> Klinger Media negotiates an agreement to purchase fifteen local newspapers around the country. The deal is reported in all of the major news publications as an illustration of the changing nature of the news business. Maria Alter, 59, knows that Klinger Media is a nonunion company and that six of the fifteen newspapers that are being acquired

have unionized employees. Since she has extensive labor relations experience, she reaches out to the company, outlining not only some of the potential issues that the company may face during the transition, but how her union experience can bring immediate value to the company related to an area with which they may not be familiar.

When reading about other companies, review every situation carefully for ways in which they could benefit from someone with your experience. That, of course, was Maria's strategy in reaching out to Klinger Media. Correctly surmising that the company was not fully equipped to handle the merging of workforces that may include unionized employees from a number of different employers, she recognized an opportunity to fill a need that the company might not even know it was going to have to address.

A FREEZE MIGHT SUGGEST ACTION

Similarly, as counterintuitive as it may sound, contacting the hiring manager at a company with a current hiring freeze can likewise yield opportunities. Just because a company stops hiring, this does not mean that their workflow slows or that the need for staff stops along with it. Besides, once the freeze is lifted the company will probably need to fill the vacancies that existed before the freeze (not to mention any new vacancies that materialized during the time of the freeze) as quickly as possible. This could result in a flood of applicants, especially if the lifting of the freeze is widely reported. By meeting with the hiring manager before the pipeline reopens, you will put yourself at the very front of the line of candidates vying for the position.

LOOK TO CREATE WIN–WIN SITUATIONS

Finally, tapping into the hidden job market can also mean creating positions that suit your needs while also addressing the needs of a prospective employer.

Charlane Green, 55, has decades of experience as a high school gym teacher in a small school. She is having difficulty finding a full-time position with a larger school district that offers a more generous salary. While she often sees part-time positions, full-time positions seem to be virtually nonexistent. Charlane decides to interview for a part-time position. When it becomes clear that the school is interested in hiring her, she suggests combining the part-time position for which she is expecting an offer with the vacancy for another position (for a part-time soccer coach), which would create a single full-time position. The school welcomes this idea, merges the two part-time positions into one full-time role, and offers her the job.

By considering the widest ranges of opportunities, and eliminating as much competition as possible once you identify them, you will put yourself in the best position for success in your job search. The hidden job market not only provides you with a new source of opportunities to target, but will likely keep you in contention for positions longer because it eliminates many of the obstacles related to your age (and how hiring managers perceive it) that prevent you from achieving your goal.

> "Talent hits a target no one else can hit; genius hits a target no one else can see."
> ARTHUR SCHOPENHAUER

YOU ARE AN EXPERIENCED CANDIDATE, NOT AN ANT

No doubt, engaging in a targeted job search that includes tapping into the hidden job market is hard. But it is also the most important job you will ever have. So, as you expend this enormous effort to research companies (both for hidden opportunities, as well as traditional ones), scour LinkedIn to develop new contacts, or rework your cover letter to paint the picture of a vibrant candidate who can hit the ground running, always remember that these are the stepping stones to achieve unprecedented success. The fact that you are working in a loyalty-free workplace and that you are an older candidate necessitates that you modify your current approach in order to achieve unprecedented success.

> "It is not enough to be busy. So are the ants. The question is: What are we busy about?"
> HENRY DAVID THOREAU

Above all, do not be discouraged by how daunting it may seem, or by the number of times you hear "no." Think about how excited everyone is when a baby takes her first steps. Does anyone ever mention the 211 times she fell to the floor before she finally made it? Of course not. Instead, they jump up and down and gloat about her success.

The same idea applies to your job search. All you need is one person or company to say "yes." So engage in a full court press and keep your eye on the ultimate prize, a job that values the wealth of experience you bring to the table and is prepared and even excited to compensate you for it.

By virtue of the fact that you are even reading this book, I know you are committed to doing whatever it takes to achieve success. Now that you know about both the obstacles that have the potential to block your path as well as the tools to maneuver around some—and get up and over others— there is no question you can get to where you need, and deserve, to go.

"As long as you are over the hill, you might as well enjoy the view."

ANONYMOUS

ACKNOWLEDGMENTS

Well, here we go again! I am so excited to have completed this new book, which builds upon the foundation I laid out in *The Perpetual Paycheck*. Once again, the level of support and guidance I received throughout this process has been incredibly humbling, with countless people responding to my seemingly never-ending requests for advice and feedback without hesitation.

First, I want to thank my family, who have always unconditionally and wholeheartedly supported me, even before they (or even I) fully understand the scope of what was ahead: my parents, Marge and Aaron; Stacey, Jeff, Logan, and Davis; Jessica, Eric, Danica, and Jamie; and Melissa and Jariel. It is difficult for me to convey my gratitude with words and you know, coming from me, that speaks volumes. Danica, Jamie, Logan, and Davis, when I wrote my first book, a textbook, you were so excited to carry it around. Now, just a few short years later, I love that you are not only carrying my books, but actually *reading* them and *editing* them to be sure that no pesky little typos fall through the cracks.

One of the biggest misconceptions about my prior book is that, in order to be successful in the loyalty-free workplace, one has to be disloyal. Speaking from experience, nothing could be farther from the truth, and I want to thank this incredible group of loyal, generous, supportive, and widely successful friends and colleagues who exemplify this: Marisol Abuin; Wade Baughman; Dave Biderman; Jen Biderman ("B"); Jayne Bower; Ann Burdick; Denise Campbell; Irene Dorzback; Marilyn Estevez; Noreen Fabre-Stahl; Sheila Garvey; Rosemary Griffin; Renee Hauch; Greg Hessinger; Ken Husserl; Harvey Jacob, Jonnathan Kessler; my penmanship consultant Onelia Lupiani Khan; Jon King; Marci, Jason, Harper, and Sloane Kroft; Sharon and Fred Kroft; Ryan Kroft and Adam Zeller; Dannielle Kyrillos; Ivy Lapides;

Kathryn Lewis; Beth Wang Llewellyn; Linda Lupiani; Maria Macca-rone; Mike McPherson; Becky Nelson; Melissa Norden; Jamie Reilly; Brett Rosenbloom; Marsha and Morey Rosenbloom; Susan Grody Ruben; Parisa Salehi; Betsy Salkind; Grace Trojanowski; Ana Venegas; Jayne Wallace; Mary Beth Wenger; and Ronnee Yashon.

And, a special thank you to my "high school" friends—Scott and Beth Atkins; Pam and Chris Brett; Terrence Donovan; Jill and John Flynn; Robyn and Dan Friedman; Tom Gatto; Kathleen Hassinger and Brandon Halbert; Caroline and Scott Heyer; Christine and Stephan Marosvary; and Tiffany Wysocki,—with whom I have been friends for decades and whose friendships I value a great deal. And, yes, in case there is any doubt, when I refer to "older job seekers," this includes us!

To my editor, Ed Robertson, thank you as always for streamlining my writing (or, as you once put it, smoothing out the icing so that the final manuscript is a perfectly frosted cake). I look forward to our continued collaborations. Thank you also to cover designer Rachel Littera, and to book designer and editor Megan Washburn for making sure that the final product that reached the hands of the readers was in its best possible shape.

In *The Perpetual Paycheck*, I paid special tribute to my friend, Judy Sand-ers, who lost her inspirational and courageous battle with cancer, but only after she overcame so many of the workplace hurdles discussed in this book. Judy, I still hear your words of wisdom, follow your advice, and know you are cheering me on. And last, but certainly not least, I wanted to remember cartoonist Randy Glasbergen, who lost his life suddenly and unexpectedly. Randy, it was an honor working with you to select the perfect cartoons for my prior books. I hope you would have approved of the selections I made here.

—Lori B. Rassas

ABOUT THE AUTHOR

The extensive practical experience Lori B. Rassas has gained as an advocate for both employers and employees in all phases of the employment relationship has led her to develop a pragmatic approach to the navigation of career issues.

Lori B. Rassas, Esq., is an SPHR-certified labor and employment attorney with close to two decades of experience. She received an LL.M in Labor and Employment Law from New York University Law School; a J.D. from George Washington University Law School; and a B.A. from Tufts University. She is a trained employment mediator and arbitrator, and has counseled employees in all phases of their careers, including individuals looking for their first jobs, individuals who have lost their jobs, and those who are changing careers. She has also advised employers on how to identify the best job candidates and build strong working relationships. Her first book, a textbook titled *Employment Law: A Guide to Hiring, Managing, and Firing for Employers and Employees* (Wolters Kluwer, 3rd ed. 2017), lays out, in clear and concise terms, much of what she has learned about the legal rights and obligations of both employers and employees. Her second book, the #1 Amazon best seller titled *The Perpetual Paycheck,* was featured on CNBC's *The Power Lunch*, and appeared in many publications, including *AARP.org, Nextavenue.org,* and *Forbes. com.* That book is a nuts-and-bolts guide to navigating the loyalty-free workplace, offering a contrarian approach backed up by actual current workplace experiences. In it, Lori provides practical, accessible job-finding secrets for those looking for a new job, those looking to solidify their current position, those looking to advance their position, and those looking to change careers or industries.

Lori currently has her own consulting practice coaching job seekers on how to effectively navigate the workplace, offering live and web-based training workshops, and providing guidance on human resources matters.

She also regularly gives career advice to students from diverse populations through her work as a member of the adjunct faculty at a number of academic institutions, including The Mailman School of Public Health of Columbia University, Fordham University School of Law, and The Scheinman Institute on Conflict Resolution at Cornell University. Lori is also a recognized expert on employment law and career issues, has appeared on CNBC, and has been quoted in a number of publications, including *The New York Times, Forbes.com, CNNMoney, Fortune, USA Today College, Newsday, American Medical News,* and *CareerBuilder.com.*

Contact Lori on LinkedIn, visit her website at *www.lorirassas.com,* follow her on Twitter (@lorirassas), or connect with her consulting practice on Facebook at www.facebook.com/loribrassas.

BEFORE YOU GO...

If you enjoyed this book, I would greatly appreciate it if you would post a short review on Amazon.com, or another online bookseller. Not only do I appreciate your support personally, but the constructive feedback I received since publishing *The Perpetual Paycheck* and *Employment Law: A Guide to Hiring, Firing, and Managing for Employers and Employees* has been an incredibly valuable tool for the publication of this book as well as for a number of other projects I have in development.

BONUS MATERIALS

As I mentioned in the introduction to this book, all of the strategies discussed in *Over the Hill But Not the Cliff* are geared towards 50+ job seekers who are looking for new opportunities in today's workplace—which by now you know is loyalty free. I first introduced this concept in *The Perpetual Paycheck: 5 Secrets to Getting a Job, Keeping a Job, and Earning Income for Life in the Loyalty-Free Workplace*, where I describe what is happening and how job seekers must modify their approach to the job search process to reflect this dramatic shift. The job search process is no longer about job candidates and their needs, but rather on the employers' needs and which job candidate is in the best position to address them. In order to achieve success in this environment, job seekers must work to exceed their employers' expectations for as long as they are rewarded for this work (in the form of growing levels of compensation). Once that compensation reaches its ceiling, the employee must look to move on to a new opportunity that will offer increasing rewards.

Given the dynamics of the loyalty-free workplace, you have to embrace the idea that your work is all about the company's needs and not about yours: We should go to work to earn the money and freedom to do the things that we want. And, if you really want to drive the engine of your dreams, it is critical to understand that workplace success begins and ends with your boss. This is the focus of Secret #2 in *The Perpetual Paycheck* (included in the pages that follow).

If you like what you have read, and would like to unearth the other four secrets to achieving unprecedented success in the loyalty-free workplace, *The Perptual Paycheck* is available on Amazon.com as a paperback, an e-book, or as an audiobook.

THE
PERPETUAL
PAYCHECK

5 Secrets to Getting a Job, Keeping a Job,
and Earning Income for Life
in the Loyalty-Free Workplace

LORI B. RASSAS

REMEMBER WHO'S BOSS

Too many people look for jobs that fit their needs. In an age of low unemployment and desperate employers, that may have made sense. But now it's all about the needs of the employer, the company, and, above all, your boss. Today the competition for jobs is fierce. Technology eliminates geographical barriers between employers and prospective applicants because web-based conferencing brings together people from all parts of the world. You need to mold yourself to fit the requirements of job opportunities, rather than wait for opportunities that fit your experiences and desires. If that means playing down your expertise and experience to get the job, so be it.

Then, once you land the job, you have to mold yourself some more to fit the needs and expectations of your boss. If you work for a 68-year-old dinosaur that wears a suit every day and responds only to written memos, you need to dress and play the part. If you're working for a 24-year-old who dresses in jeans and communicates only via text, buy some flip-flops and limber up your thumbs. Whatever your attire, when you make your boss shine, you'll almost immediately see rewards beyond what you ever imagined.

A boss starts his weekly staff meeting by thanking his employees for participating in the recent brainstorming exercises and providing him with constructive feedback on how to improve his management style. He particularly appreciates the suggestion of one particular employee, Eric, that he lighten up and incorporate more humor into his daily interactions with the staff.

Wasting no time, the boss asks Eric to stand.

"Knock, knock," said the boss.

"Who's there?" replies Eric.

"Not you for much longer," says the boss.

—UNKNOWN

Make no mistake about it: Your paycheck and your business card may have the company's name on it, but you work for your boss. He has the power in the relationship—and in the loyalty-free workplace, your success at your job depends on your ability to make that relationship work.

First, your boss has significant control over the terms and conditions of your current employment. He is responsible for completing your performance evaluations, which often serve as the basis for your level of compensation. Most companies will offer you a raise, provided your boss agrees that your work is satisfactory and benefits the company. Conversely, few companies will approve your raise if your boss opposes it.

Second, the more you get along with your boss, the better your chances of advancing your career. Since your boss likely assigns your day-to-day tasks, you'll want to be sure that he has confidence in you and assigns you work of increasing complexity. That way, you will develop skills that make you more marketable for future opportunities, which will enable you to earn enhanced levels of compensation.

Finally, for better or for worse, your reputation at work begins and ends with your boss. How he speaks about your work to others can help or hinder you as you pursue other opportunities. He also may have access to information that you may find useful, not to mention connections to people whose paths you may not otherwise cross.

Navigating one's relationship with the boss requires a practical approach. That can be hard to do sometimes, because it goes against human nature to build relationships with people we may not necessarily like. However, if you really think about it, we often enter into relationships with people, regardless of our personal feelings toward them, because we think we can benefit from that relationship. You may despise a certain real estate broker, but if that broker has the exclusive listings for apartments in a building where you want to live, you'll put your personal feelings aside and work with him. In some cases, we don't recognize the problem until after we've started the relationship. You may have liked your landlord when you signed a one-year lease, only to find him to be meddlesome six months later. Or you may decide, halfway into building a new addition to your home, that you went with the wrong general contractor. In each of these scenarios, you weigh your dissatisfaction with the relationship against the consequences of disrupting it.

Sometimes, though, we may stay in a less than ideal relationship, even if nothing prevents us from leaving it. For example, if your marriage is no longer working, rather than file for divorce right away, you may choose to remain married until your children are grown or your finances are in order. In other words, we muddle through the circumstances for as long as we need to.

> A boss starts out his weekly staff meeting with his regular joke. The entire team started to laugh, except for one employee.
>
> "What's your problem?" asks the boss. "Don't you think I am funny?"
>
> "I no longer have to think you are funny," the employee replies. "Friday is my last day."
>
> —UNKNOWN

Because we work for money and for advancement in the loyalty-free workplace, we do the best we can to earn as much as we can, then move on to whatever is next.

FIGURE OUT HOW YOUR BOSS WORKS

The key to establishing a strong relationship with your boss is to determine what makes that manager tick. A very wise colleague of mine used to remind me, "Sometimes you are the hammer, sometimes you are the nail." Meaning, there will always be instances where your boss will want you to take the lead and complete the project as you see fit. At the same time, there will also be occasions when it's best to fly under the radar and do what your boss says (regardless of whether you agree with him or not).

> "Sometimes you are the hammer, sometimes you are the nail."
> **UNKNOWN**

How do you learn the difference? By getting to know your boss' personality and adapting your behavior accordingly. In the loyalty-free workplace, that's what it's all about.

Alexander McKinley, 31, is an employee benefit advisor who is thrilled to have landed a job with a bottling company. On his first day of work, Alexander eagerly shows up a half hour early. Dressed in a pin-striped suit and carrying a briefcase, he waits in the reception area for the others to arrive. The receptionist arrives at 9:00am sharp. Alexander's boss, Lynne Borne, 55, arrives at 9:10am, but as she's late for her 9:00am conference call, she immediately closes her office door. After knocking on Lynne's door, Alexander informs her that he will wait for his first assignment in his office down the hall.

Alexander's employment with the bottling company lasted just seven weeks. Let's just say that his relationship with Lynne went downhill from the moment he arrived. Having come from a corporate environment, Alexander wanted his boss to adapt to

> "A power struggle with your boss is when she has the power and you have the struggle."
> **ANONYMOUS**

his needs, instead of the other way around. That was unfortunate, because he could have averted the entire disaster with a few small modifications.

Alexander lamented Lynne's absence of organization skills and, particularly, her refusal to let him create a simple filing system to track benefit changes. When Lynne asked him to tell her how many benefit complaints were logged in a particular month, he provided her with an itemized spreadsheet that analyzed the type of complaints, when they were filed, and their current status. When Lynne placed Alexander on a performance management plan and told him that his job performance had to improve if he expected to continue to work in the office, Alexander started to work nights and weekends, thoroughly answering emails while copying Lynne on his responses.

It didn't take long for me to peg Lynne's personality: She did not want an organizational system or a detailed spreadsheet, and she certainly didn't want to hear from Alexander on the weekends. Lynne wanted what she

> "Don't set your own rules when you are someone's guest."
> **ITALIAN PROVERB**

wanted when she wanted it, and Alexander should have figured out how to give her what she wanted, in the simplest way possible. When Lynne asked how many complaints were filed, Alexander should have responded with a single number. When she wanted a file, he should have pulled his copy from his own files and handed it to her.

SOME GENERATIONAL GUIDANCE

Need help assessing your boss' style? Here are a few guidelines.

IF YOUR BOSS WAS BORN BETWEEN 1946 AND 1964, HE IS LIKELY A BABY BOOMER AND THEREFORE

- defines himself by his career, earns a lot of money, and is in a position of authority
- believes hard work produces tangible rewards
- requires "face time," and disapproves of arrangements that permit employees to complete their work from remote locations

IF YOUR BOSS WAS BORN BETWEEN 1965 AND 1980, HE IS LIKELY A GENERATION Xer, AND THEREFORE

- is independent, self-sufficient, comfortable with technology, and committed to achieving great success—but on his own terms
- is inclined to admit a lack of loyalty to his employer
- sees the importance of a personal life over a career

IF YOUR BOSS WAS BORN IN THE 1980s OR LATER, HE IS LIKELY A GENERATION Yer (OR CONSIDERS HIMSELF TO BE A "MILLENNIAL") AND THEREFORE

- is connected to technology 24/7 (and, therefore, prefers to communicate and learn through technology, as opposed to more traditional face-to-face interactions)
- values his personal life over his professional life and will sacrifice rigorous employment situations for a more robust personal life
- is achievement-oriented and expects the company to provide assistance in reaching his goals
- is not afraid to challenge authority
- expects workplace feedback and rewards for his work

Still not sure? Then simply ask your boss what best suits his needs (for example, "Should I give updates as I make progress with a project, or would you rather I update you at our monthly staff meetings?").

If you're like most people, it may take a few interactions before you can appropriately characterize your boss, plus you'll likely gather more information as your relationship evolves. It doesn't matter how you manage to pinpoint his style, so long as you do it.

DON'T TRY TO CHANGE YOUR BOSS—PICK YOUR BATTLES INSTEAD

Let's say you've nailed down your boss' personality, but you still find him difficult to manage. Should you reach out for help? Yes, but tread carefully. In the loyalty-free workplace, there is no guarantee that the process you use or the information you share will remain confidential.

Besides, unless the situation is extreme (such as an issue of safety or discrimination), it's entirely possible that the problem is not with your boss, but with your expectations. Meaning, assuming your boss is an adult with a fully developed personality, certain aspects of his behavior are unlikely to change. In that case, your best bet is to work things out with your supervisor, rather than to go over his head.

Lucinda Alverez, 49, was the assistant manager of a national hotel chain. She worked for the general manager, Brian Curtail, 54. Brian was known for micromanaging his employees and not allowing anyone to make their own decisions. After Lucinda returned from a business trip meeting with the directors of each of the regional offices, Brian summoned her to his office for a full debrief. Lucinda said that she was able to close all of the deals as instructed, "including having the fully executed agreement from the western region, despite the arrogance of that group's director." When Brian asked her to elaborate, Lucinda explained that the director signed the agreement, even though he felt that "corporate greed was taking advantage of the regional centers." Though Lucinda indicated that several other offices expressed similar sentiments, she also told Brian that this was a non-issue.

Before Lucinda knew it, Brian had put his phone on speaker and started dialing the direct line for the director of the western region. Though Lucinda implored Brian not to intervene, he merely waved his hands and told her, "I'll handle it." When the director answered, Brian said, "I have Lucinda Alvarez with me. She tells me you were rude and out of line when you spoke to her. I think you should apologize." The director immediately apologized and insisted that he did not intend to disrespect Lucinda in any way. With that, Brian ended the call and told Lucinda that she did a great job.

Needless to say, Lucinda was completely embarrassed by Brian's actions and wanted my advice on how to handle it. Unfortunately, in a situation like this, where the boss is a fifty-four-year-old middle manager whose penchant for micromanaging is not going to change, the only appropriate response is to make a mental note of it, and move on.

Look at it this way. Being a micromanager, it's Brian's style to get involved with everything. Lucinda knows this, so what did she expect to gain by bringing this to his attention?

"If we want to succeed as a team, we need to put aside our own selfish, individual interests and start doing things my way."

> "Parenting Tip: Treat a difficult child the way you would your boss at work. Praise his achievements, ignore his tantrums and resist the urge to sit him down and explain to him how his brain is not yet fully developed."
>
> **ROBERT BRAULT**

Now, let's say that, after the phone call to the western region, Lucinda told Brian that she wished he would've handled the situation differently. Best case, Brian would have actively listened to Lucinda's concerns and altered his future behavior. The problem is, being a micromanager Brian would have also felt compelled to do something about it such as picking up the phone, making another call to the western director, and trying to undo the situation. All that would have done was make Lucinda even more embarrassed.

You'll notice that I did not suggest that Lucinda just move on—instead, I suggested she make a mental note of it and move on. After all, her embarrassment aside, the situation actually provided a wealth of information that Lucinda can use to her advantage. For one, she now knows that, if she doesn't want Brian to be involved in a particular matter, she should keep it to herself. Conversely, if she does want him to intervene, all she has to do is say it. More to the point, Lucinda also now knows that Brian likes her work. Whatever she's doing, she should keep doing

> "The shortest and best way to make your fortune is to let people see clearly that it is in their interest to promote yours."
>
> **JEAN DE LA BRUYERE**

it. Remember this is a boss-employee relationship and therefore, by definition, it is about her boss. Lucinda now basically has a road map as to how Brian will handle what he sees as inappropriate behavior. It is not up to Lucinda to change his response; instead it is up to Lucinda to modify her behavior in response to it.

HOW DO YOU HANDLE A NARCISSISTIC BOSS? BY MANAGING UP

In the loyalty-free workplace, you have to keep your boss happy. That can be tricky if your boss happens to be a narcissist. After all, to a narcissist, everything is about them—you can't expect them to reward you for your accomplishments, no matter how hard you try.

> WHEN YOU MANAGE UP, YOU MOVE UP.

Yet, even a narcissistic boss can be handled successfully, so long as you separate yourself from the narcissistic personality. Meaning, if a narcissist subjects you to unwarranted harsh criticism, remember the harshness is more about them than it is about you. One effective way to effectively manage this situation is to manage up.

Managing up simply means to work according to this credo: "When the boss looks good, you look good." By making your boss look good, you establish trust and good will with him. Therefore, anything that reflects favorably on your boss will reflect favorably on you.

> A boss takes his employee for a ride in his new car.
>
> "Wow! This is an amazing car," says the employee.
>
> "It certainly is," says the boss. "And if you exceed this year's goals more than you exceeded last year's goals, then next year I will get an even better one."
>
> —UNKNOWN

The fact is, when you manage up, you make yourself indispensable to your boss. That can provide you with some degree of job security as you look for your next opportunity.

RESPECT THE ROLE

To effectively manage up, you have to understand that your job is to help your boss with his work, and not create more work for him by being difficult to manage.

Ana Bellingers, 23, is a recent college graduate. While dining out with her parents, Ana is asked whether she will have trouble getting time off for her cousin's upcoming out-of-town wedding. "Of course not," she replies. "This is my cousin's wedding, so I am going. I don't need to ask my boss for time off. I just need to inform her that I will be out of the office."

Being a typical Millennial, Ana tends to value her personal life over her professional life. That's fine if she happens to work for herself—but she doesn't. She has a boss, and she needs to remember that if she wants to keep her job and keep herself in the best position to increase the size of her paycheck.

> "A company hires you to resolve company problems, not to be the problem of the company."
>
> **UNKNOWN**

In the loyalty-free workplace, your boss is still your boss, and you have to respect their role. That means reporting to work on time, requesting permission to work different hours if you have a doctor's appointment, and asking for approval if you want certain days off. That also means making your boss' life as easy as possible. Your boss doesn't want to walk into the office wondering whether you're going to do your job that day, or if he still has a customer base because he hired you.

I once received a call from a very successful dentist who asked if I knew anyone who might be interested in working as an office manager. When I asked him about the qualifications for the position, he said, "All I want is someone who will show up to work on time." When I asked if he could expand on that, he explained that while all of his prior office managers came highly recommended, they each also ended up hurting his business, despite being good at their job. In one case, the manager had a habit of sharing too much information. For example, one day she called in sick.

> "Don't broadcast your troubles. There's no market for them."
>
> **UNKNOWN**

When she returned to work the following day, the dentist asked how she was feeling. The manager proceeded to tell him at length about how her virus was related to her stomach problems, vomiting, and what she'd been eating for the past two days. Unfortunately for the dentist, this exchange happened to take place in the reception area, in front of several waiting patients.

Does this mean that you should never share any personal issues with your boss? Not necessarily. You are only human and you will likely want to establish some type of personal connection. But there's a time and a place for everything. If your boss asks you to get Mrs. Klein's x-rays, or is waiting for you to format the PowerPoint slides for his upcoming presentation to the board of directors, the last thing he wants to hear at that moment is about your break-up, financial difficulties, problems with the mover, or what you had for dinner last night that made you so terribly sick.

Remember your boss has a job to do, too. While managing you is part of that job, it shouldn't take up so much of his time that it prevents him from getting his own work done. If it does, he will find someone else.

Does managing up mean you should be a brownnoser or a sycophant? No. But it does mean equipping your boss with the information he needs to do his job effortlessly and effectively. Remember, by making your boss look indispensable, you've made yourself indispensable, too.

Now what if your boss has a reputation for being unprepared in meet-ings, or does not come across well or command any respect? That could reflect poorly on you. If this is the case, it's even more imperative that you manage up. By looking out for your boss, you are also looking out for yourself. In the loyalty-free workplace, no one is going to reach out to you and give you a reward. If you want to be acknowledged, you have to assert your relevance to your boss and, when practical, to others around you.

BE PROACTIVE: ANTICIPATE YOUR BOSS' NEEDS

Another benefit of managing up: By showing others that you and your boss can handle challenging tasks, they will not only value your expertise, but know that they can rely on you to get the work done with little to no interference. Your boss will appreciate that, because it shows he knows how to manage effectively to produce impressive results. But that also benefits you by providing a semblance of job security, even in a loyalty-free workplace. For example, in the event the company faces reorganization that will include layoffs, your boss will keep your name out of those conversations—if only because it's in *his* best interest to ensure you remain at his side.

> "Above all, be loyal to your superior's agenda."
>
> **JOHN DELOREAN**
>
> BUSINESSMAN SUMMARIZING THE CORPORATE PHILOSOPHY OF ROGER SMITH, CEO OF GENERAL MOTORS

Remember, the best employees manage themselves—they report to work on time and are where they need to be. Along the same lines, prospective employers can usually gauge what type of employee you might be during the interview process. If you show up for the interview on time and ready to go, you stand a much better chance of getting hired than someone who needs to reschedule an interview three times, or who arrives late or unprepared.

Say you have a friend who is coping with an aging parent or a seriously ill child. If you're like most people, you may send flowers or tell them, "Anything you need, just ask." While those gestures are certainly appreciated, the ones that really stand out are when you empty your friend's dishwasher and take out the trash.

You should approach your relationship with your boss in much the same way. Besides making yourself easy to manage, let your boss know that you're ready to help when he needs it—and act on it when he asks. If she's overwhelmed with an upcoming presentation, offer to draft some of the more mundane parts of the presentation, or perhaps to format the slides. Even if she says no, she will remember that you were willing to support her when she needed it. That will serve you well in the end.

SMARTER IS BETTER

What if you think you're more qualified than your boss, or believe you deserve some of the credit that he receives? For one, this is not a bad place to be, and you wouldn't be alone—many successful executives hire team members who are smart and talented, especially in areas where they do not excel, because they know they can make them shine. That being the case, it becomes even more imperative that you manage up. After all, since your boss has no loyalty, he is less likely to support you as his career takes off if he knows you're not there for his best interests—whereas, when your boss knows you're there for him, he might tell the senior executives that you're the best person to succeed him in his current position when he leaves for another company. It could also mean creating a spot for you at a higher level when he moves to another company and is charged with hiring a new team.

> " Always be smarter than the people who hire you. "
> **LENA HORNE**

This brings us to another point. Part of managing up is learning about the goals of your boss and helping him achieve them. Not only will that cement your relationship, it will help your boss earn a promotion which, in turn, can help you advance your career.

The same holds true for issues related to compensation. Whether you like your boss or can't stand him, it's in your best interest to help him earn a raise. If your boss gets a raise, you'll likely get one, too. But if his salary is frozen because he's on a performance management plan, guess what? Your chances for a salary increase will likewise be affected.

And when the time comes to ask for a raise (or any other personal request), don't just say, "I'd like more money every week." Instead, phrase it in a way that makes it seem like you're helping your boss as well. If you need to earn a certain level of income in order for the job to be an option (or would like the company to pay for a course in continuing education), emphasize the skills that you bring to work every day and how that will continue to benefit the company. Similarly, if you need to adjust your work schedule because of personal obligations, present the request in terms of how this will "maximize your productivity at the office."

ENOUGH ABOUT YOUR BOSS, MORE ABOUT YOUR BOSS

In the loyalty-free workplace, a shrewd employee can get what he wants so long as the employer also gets what *they* want in return.

> Bob Ashwell, 36, works for a company that is hosting a retreat to celebrate the launch of a new bicycle. As part of his job, Bob is expected to lead one of the groups through a bike tour. The weekend before the convention Bob breaks his ankle and will therefore be unable to participate in the ride.

> Bob's boss decides to replace him at the retreat with another employee who was not originally scheduled to attend. Bob strenuously objects to his boss' decision to exclude him from the event and wants to discuss the matter further.

Even though he couldn't lead the bike ride as previously planned, Bob still wanted to attend the retreat because he saw it as a valuable opportunity to network with staff members from other parts of the country. Just as important, he was concerned that his absence from the event would reflect badly on him at the office. To resolve the situation, he prepared a memo to his boss outlining the reasons he felt it was important for him to be there.

First, Bob explained he planned to meet with a number of people at the convention to resolve some challenging issues that, for one reason or another, had stalled. Many of these matters involved personnel from other regional officers who were attending the event. By meeting these parties face to face, Bob felt that he could resolve these matters efficiently, without the company incurring the costs of multiple overnight trips. In addition, knowing that the company would have a business office set up for use by the attendees, Bob offered to relieve the administrative assistant of her responsibilities during the bike tour—that way, he could oversee the office, while the administrative assistant led the bike ride.

After reviewing the memo, Bob's boss reconsidered his decision and permitted Bob to attend the event within the parameters he outlined. The key for Bob was identifying his needs first, and then presenting them in a manner that met the needs of his employer.

> Advertising executive Ann Garrity, 37, is about to return from her maternity leave. Though she knows that she is a valued employee, her company is facing a one-year wage freeze. Ann would like to work from home at least one day a week so that she can spend more time with her newborn and avoid the grueling 70-mile daily commute. She is about to discuss these matters with her boss, but does not believe her scheduled call will go well.

Ann first came to me with the idea of changing jobs. After a brief discussion, we both agreed that it would be better for her if she remained in her current position with new terms, at least for the time being. The question was how to broach the matter with her boss.

Ann's initial plan was to be very direct—she wanted to work from home to spend more time with her children and less time commuting to and from work. In other words, "This is my need, and this is what benefits me." The problem with that approach, of course, is twofold. If her employer is like most companies, they will probably worry that if she works from home, any time she spends with her baby may impair her ability to do her job. And as for her commuting costs, her boss will likely tell Ann, "That's your problem, not mine."

However, with a few adjustments, Ann presented her request in a way that benefited her *and* her employer. For one, she said that she'd agree to the one-year salary freeze in exchange for working from home twice a week. This arrangement would offset the money she'd need to continue to fill her gas tank. In addition, knowing that the company recently rented office space on another floor to accommodate the growing staff, she suggested that she share her office with another employee who is offered a similar arrangement. That would save the company the additional cost of at least one office on another floor.

Not only did Ann's boss accept this arrangement, but he applauded her for coming up with a creative way of addressing the company's financial pressures without impacting any of its clients. While Ann's income won't grow for the next twelve months, she will save money in commuting costs every month, not to mention spare herself of six hours of driving per week—time that she can spend with her family, or looking for her next job.

> "Office politics is just like the lottery. Dreaming about winning doesn't get you anywhere—there's no payoff if you don't buy a ticket. You have to play if you want to win."
>
> **JAMIE FABIAN**

Now, you may ask, "If it's all about addressing the needs of the boss, aren't we being disingenuous when we seek out mutual benefits?" The answer to that is no. After all, employers engage in the same behavior all the time in the loyalty-free workplace. A wise employee keeps that in mind when discussing the terms and conditions of employment.

I once had a client who landed a coveted job at a large power company. He was quite proud of the fact that he was assigned the largest office in the building, which included a plush couch, a private bathroom, and even his own shower. Naturally, he saw those perks as an indication of how much the company valued him. What he didn't realize was that, by lavishing him with the comforts of home, the company was expecting him to put in longer days at the office. Why bother going home to get a few hours of sleep and a shower, when he could merely take a quick nap in his office, shower, and be ready to go back to work?

Few people would ever agree to work twenty-hour days. But you might be more willing to spend many more nights at the office (as this client did), if it meant getting a large office with your own bathroom in return.

The point is, when you manage up, you can put yourself in a position to advance your career, while also making your boss shine.

NEVER TAKE A JOB BASED ON WHO YOU THINK YOU'LL BE WORKING FOR

So far we've talked about how to handle an actual boss. Now let's take a look at how to handle a prospective boss.

What if you learn that you're about to be reassigned to the proverbial Boss from Hell—a complete jerk who goes through assistants like Kleenex because he runs them ragged? Do you start sending out resumes or call your friend the recruiter? Or what if you've interviewed for a position that seems like a perfect fit—you meet the qualifications, the work atmosphere is friendly and easygoing, and the boss is an absolute dream?

In both scenarios, you have to remember that the rules of the loyalty-free workplace apply to everyone. No one's tenure is any more guaranteed than yours. Therefore, whether your prospective boss has a fantastic reputation or a lousy one, you should never base an employment decision on for whom you *think* you'll be working. Why? Because the people to whom you're actually reporting can change at a moment's notice.

> A single mom stuck in a dead end job with a government agency, Marnie Maynard, 31, interviewed for a position with a non-profit agency. Many people warned her about the excessive red tape at the organization, and that her prospective boss was known to be a very unstable woman. When she interviewed, however, Marnie found that, due to a reorganization, she would be reporting to the head of the department—a man who was not only well-respected, but could be an invaluable resource. The red tape, however, was not an exaggeration. Though Marnie originally interviewed for the position in November, it would be four months before she finally received the job offer in March. She would not start in the new position until May 1st.

Unfortunately for Marnie, on her first day of work, she learned that the man who was supposed to be her boss was reassigned to a new position.

Naturally, Marnie was distraught—especially once she learned that the new head of the department was the very same woman that she had been told to avoid. However, just two months later, she had a happy ending: The troublesome woman resigned, leaving Marnie with an entirely different job and reporting structure than what had been originally contemplated. The point is, nothing in the loyalty-free workplace is guaranteed. That goes for the benefits of the position (such as continued job security) and the drawbacks (a less than ideal boss).

BEWARE OF INFORMATION FROM THIRD PARTIES

Remember, too, that everyone puts his best foot forward during an interview, including the interviewer. So even if you develop a bond with a potential boss during the interview process, that may not reflect how she would behave in other situations. Further, even if your prospective boss seems incredibly inspiring during the interview process, she may not be as inspiring when handling her daily supervisory responsibilities.

Besides, what you hear about a prospective boss may not reflect reality. As the saying goes, no matter how flat you make a pancake, it still has two sides.

> David Aarons, 26, is a recent law school graduate looking for a job. He has heard many horror stories about law firm partners who torment their junior associates as part of the process to initiate them into the practice of law. After interviewing with one law firm partner, David sees no red flags but is taken aback by the candor of the two other associates who speak to him as part of the interview process. Both junior associates tell David that the partner is difficult to work with, and they recount situations where they received emails in the middle of the night, with aggressive deadlines that came and went even before they woke up to read the original email.

They also speak of being chastised in large group meetings, low employee morale, and the high turnover rate (which they say accounts for the current vacancy).

David then speaks with a law school career counselor who emphasizes the importance of finding a first job in a supportive environment. Based on that conversation, David decides not to work at that particular law firm, even before learning whether an offer would have been made.

Not only did David opt out of the interview process without even knowing the terms of any offer he might have received (or even confirming what supervisory structure might have been in place), he based his decision on the input of two employees with whom he had no prior history.

Most employees know better than to speak negatively of their supervisors, particularly at a time when their current income depends on the continuation of that relationship. For all David knew, these two associates may have been so distraught over their current employment status that they no longer cared about their utter lack of professionalism.

Then again, one imagines that the associates may have had some ulterior motivations for sharing negative information with David. (As it happens, a few years after that interview, David learned that the firm filled the position by hiring an associate that had previously worked for the firm.) While there's no way to confirm this, it's entirely possible that the two associates had another friend whom they wanted to see hired instead of David—in which case, it would have been in their best interest to dissuade David, and any other candidates, from pursuing the job. It's also possible, given the competitive nature of the loyalty-free workplace, that the associates simply viewed the hiring of an additional associate as a threat to their future employment.

> "No matter how flat you make a pancake, it still has two sides."
> **DR. PHIL**

The point is, third parties in the interview process—that is to say, people whom you may meet in the course of the interview, but who have no bearing whatsoever in the final decision—may act in a way to impact the process. Your job is to determine whether they're giving you useful information, or not. What's the difference? Useful information is that which ultimately helps you achieve your end goal, which is to earn a growing and perpetual paycheck.

Let's consider another example:

> Madeline Deveer, 42, applied for a job as a patient service representative at a large city hospital. After meeting with her prospective boss (who had no reservations about Madeline's ability to work for her), Madeline met with several other hospital employees as part of the interview process. One employee, Edwin Gainer, 36, suggests that Madeline's prospective boss would be challenging to work with. Although Edwin did not provide any additional details, it was clear to Madeline that he was discouraging her from taking the job. Though Madeline gave Edwin's comments some thought, when she was offered the position—at a salary that was considerably higher than her current job—and she accepted the offer.
>
> Madeline ended up thriving in her new position and established an excellent rapport with her boss.

When Madeline accepted the position, she did not know any specific details about the relationship between Edwin and her future boss. But, as far as Madeline is concerned, it didn't matter. Her only goal is the same as yours: to maintain a stream of income and, ideally, to increase that stream of income over time. Of course you want to enter into a new situation with your eyes open, but *you* want to be the one making the decision.

It turned out that four years after Madeline started working for the company, she learned that her boss and Edwin had once been romantically involved, and that their relationship ended badly. This certainly explained the feelings of animosity Edwin may have had toward her boss. Even still, had she known that information at the time the offer was presented, it still should not have had any impact on her decision.

> "The handwriting on the wall may be a forgery."
>
> **RALPH HODGSON**
> ENGLISH POET

Remember, the ultimate goal is to get a promotion that offers you more compensation. If working at the hospital for Edwin's former girlfriend helps Madeline reach that goal, then she should accept the offer. If it doesn't, then she should look for the next opportunity.

Along the same lines, just as you should never dismiss a great opportunity because of the potential for a terrible boss, don't be afraid to pursue opportunities for advancement (and a larger paycheck), no matter how amazing your current boss is. In the loyalty-free workplace, you must always look out for yourself.

> Gary Anderson, 56, works as an architect in a corporate development firm. Gary performs a lot of work behind the scenes, for which his boss, Lenny Hart (also 56), receives credit. In return, Lenny uses his influence to ensure that Gary receives challenging work and significant salary increases.
>
> When Gary is approached by a recruiter about a ground-floor opportunity at a new firm that offers a significant salary increase, he declines to even meet with the recruiter to discuss the position, out of loyalty to Lenny. Six months later, however, Lenny announces he is leaving the company to work for a competing development firm. When Lenny's replacement is hired, he has a new vision for the department. As a result, Gary finds himself out of a job.

In this case, Gary lost sight of the reason for all of his hard work: to qualify for promotional opportunities. At the very least, he should have talked to the recruiter about the new opportunity, even though accepting it would have required him to leave the solid working relationship he had developed with Lenny. Besides, if Gary could successfully "manage up" one boss, he should be able to do the same with the next one.

> "Would I ever leave this company? Look, I'm all about loyalty. In fact, I feel like part of what I'm being paid for here is my loyalty. But if there were somewhere else that valued loyalty more highly, I'm going wherever they value loyalty the most."
>
> **DWIGHT SCHRUTE**
> FROM THE TELEVISION SHOW THE OFFICE

No doubt, there are incredible bosses, just as there are terrible bosses. But all bosses have to make tough decisions sometimes, especially in the loyalty-free workplace. Gary may have loved Lenny, but if Lenny had been forced to lay Gary off while he was still paying college tuition for his two children, he may think differently.

Remember, too, that because the workplace is loyalty-free, at some point your boss may have to make decisions that are in his best interest and perhaps not in yours. Say you're in the break room, having an animated conversation with a coworker. You raise your voice and make an innocuous comment in jest. The coworker, however, feels threatened by your comment, and files a formal complaint. Even though the boss knows that you were just being funny (and doesn't see you as a threat at all), depending on the circumstances, he may have to impose disciplinary action.

This goes back to the point we made in our earlier example with Marnie: Never make a workplace decision based on your current boss. In the loyalty-free workplace, that sort of information can change on a moment's notice (as Gary learned the hard way).

YOU CAN'T CONTROL ANY MOVEMENT OTHER THAN YOUR OWN

In a loyalty-free workplace, there are no guarantees. We can't expect any aspect of our employment, or that of our boss or coworkers, to remain the same. All we can do is work as best we can in the circumstances in which we find ourselves, no matter what those circumstances are.

While this may seem daunting at first, it really isn't once you stop and think about it. After all, everyone is in the same boat, and the tide can turn before you know it. Knowing that, a smart employee will continue to earn his perpetual and growing paycheck by accepting the importance of getting along with his boss, whoever that is, at any given time.

When you manage up, you move up. Once you master how that works, it will not matter who your boss is, because you'll know that you can successfully implement this strategy over and over again. Keep in mind that even if you are effectively managing your boss, the rewards may not be immediate. In fact, it is inevitable that there will be times when you do not receive the results you desire, or that it will seem like everyone else is moving upward and onward and you are standing still. The good news is that even when you are faced with what seems like a dire situation, there are almost always hidden benefits that can be easily claimed. This is the focus of secret number three.

CPSIA information can be obtained
at www.ICGtesting.com
Printed in the USA
LVHW040241150420
653511LV00020B/3294